MW00464975

PHRASEBOOK

— ALBANIAN —

THE MOST
IMPORTANT
PHRASES

This phrasebook contains
the most important
phrases and questions
for basic communication
Everything you need
to survive overseas

BOOKS

By Andrey Taranov

English-Albanian phrasebook & concise dictionary

By Andrey Taranov

The collection of "Everything Will Be Okay" travel phrasebooks published by T&P Books is designed for people traveling abroad for tourism and business. The phrasebooks contain what matters most - the essentials for basic communication. This is an indispensable set of phrases to "survive" while abroad.

Another section of the book also provides a small dictionary with more than 1,500 useful words arranged alphabetically. The dictionary includes a lot of gastronomic terms and will be helpful when ordering food at a restaurant or buying groceries at the store.

T&P Books Publishing
www.tpbooks.com

ISBN: 978-1-78767-150-8

This book is also available in E-book formats.
Please visit www.tpbooks.com or the major online bookstores.

FOREWORD

The collection of "Everything Will Be Okay" travel phrasebooks published by T&P Books is designed for people traveling abroad for tourism and business. The phrasebooks contain what matters most - the essentials for basic communication. This is an indispensable set of phrases to "survive" while abroad.

This phrasebook will help you in most cases where you need to ask something, get directions, find out how much something costs, etc. It can also resolve difficult communication situations where gestures just won't help.

This book contains a lot of phrases that have been grouped according to the most relevant topics. A separate section of the book also provides a small dictionary with more than 1,500 important and useful words.

Take "Everything Will Be Okay" phrasebook with you on the road and you'll have an irreplaceable traveling companion who will help you find your way out of any situation and teach you to not fear speaking with foreigners.

TABLE OF CONTENTS

T&P Books Publishing

PRONUNCIATION

T&P phonetic alphabet	Albanian example	English example
[a]	flas [flas]	shorter than in ask
[e], [ɛ]	melodi [mɛlodí]	absent, pet
[ə]	kërkoj [kərkój]	driver, teacher
[i]	pikë [píkə]	shorter than in feet
[o]	motor [motór]	pod, John
[u]	fuqi [fucí]	book
[y]	myshk [myʃk]	fuel, tuna
[b]	brakë [brákə]	baby, book
[c]	oqean [ocɛán]	Irish - ceist
[d]	adoptoj [adoptój]	day, doctor
[dz]	lexoj [lɛdzój]	beads, kids
[dʒ]	xham [dʒam]	joke, general
[ð]	dhomë [ðómə]	weather, together
[f]	i fortë [i fórtə]	face, food
[g]	bullgari [bułgarí]	game, gold
[h]	jaht [jáht]	home, have
[j]	hyrje [hýrjɛ]	yes, New York
[ɟ]	zgjedh [zɟɛð]	geese
[k]	korik [korík]	clock, kiss
[l]	lëviz [ləvíz]	lace, people
[ɫ]	shkallë [ʃkáɫə]	feel
[m]	medalje [mɛdáljɛ]	magic, milk
[n]	klan [klan]	name, normal
[ɲ]	spanjoll [spaɲóɫ]	canyon, new
[ŋ]	trung [truŋ]	ring
[p]	polici [politsí]	pencil, private
[r]	i erët [i érət]	rice, radio
[ɾ]	groshë [gróʃə]	Spanish - pero
[s]	spital [spitál]	city, boss
[ʃ]	shes [ʃɛs]	machine, shark
[t]	tapet [tapét]	tourist, trip
[ts]	batica [batítsa]	cats, tsetse fly
[tʃ]	kaçube [katʃúbɛ]	church, French
[v]	javor [javór]	very, river
[z]	horizont [horizónt]	zebra, please
[ʒ]	kuzhinë [kuʒínə]	forge, pleasure
[θ]	përkthej [pərkθéj]	month, tooth

5

LIST OF ABBREVIATIONS

English abbreviations

ab.	-	about
adj	-	adjective
adv	-	adverb
anim.	-	animate
as adj	-	attributive noun used as adjective
e.g.	-	for example
etc.	-	et cetera
fam.	-	familiar
fem.	-	feminine
form.	-	formal
inanim.	-	inanimate
masc.	-	masculine
math	-	mathematics
mil.	-	military
n	-	noun
pl	-	plural
pron.	-	pronoun
sb	-	somebody
sing.	-	singular
sth	-	something
v aux	-	auxiliary verb
vi	-	intransitive verb
vi, vt	-	intransitive, transitive verb
vt	-	transitive verb

Albanian abbreviations

f	-	feminine noun
m	-	masculine noun
pl	-	plural

ALBANIAN
PHRASEBOOK

This section contains
important phrases that may
come in handy in various
real-life situations.
The phrasebook will help
you ask for directions, clarify
a price, buy tickets, and
order food at a restaurant

T&P Books Publishing

PHRASEBOOK
CONTENTS

T&P Books Publishing

Excuse me, …	**Më falni, …** [mə fálni, …]
Hello.	**Përshëndetje.** [pərʃəndétjɛ]
Thank you.	**Faleminderit.** [falɛmindérit]
Good bye.	**Mirupafshim.** [mirupáfʃim]
Yes.	**Po.** [po]
No.	**Jo.** [jo]
I don't know.	**Nuk e di.** [nuk ɛ di]
Where? | Where to? | When?	**Ku? | Për ku? | Kur?** [ku? | pər ku? | kur?]

I need …	**Më nevojitet …** [mə nɛvojítɛt …]
I want …	**Dua …** [dúa …]
Do you have …?	**Keni …?** [kéni …?]
Is there a … here?	**A ka … këtu?** [a ka … kətú?]
May I …?	**Mund të …?** [mund tə …?]
…, please (polite request)	**…, ju lutem** […], [ju lútɛm]

I'm looking for …	**Kërkoj …** [kərkój …]
the restroom	**tualet** [tualét]
an ATM	**bankomat** [bankomát]
a pharmacy (drugstore)	**farmaci** [farmatsí]
a hospital	**spital** [spitál]
the police station	**komisariat policie** [komisariát politsíɛ]
the subway	**metro** [mɛtró]

a taxi	**taksi** [táksi]
the train station	**stacion treni** [statsión trɛni]

My name is …	**Më quajnë …** [mə cúajnə …]
What's your name?	**Si quheni?** [si cúhɛni?]
Could you please help me?	**Ju lutem, mund të ndihmoni?** [ju lútɛm], [mund tə ndihmóni?]
I've got a problem.	**Kam një problem.** [kam ɲə problém]
I don't feel well.	**Nuk ndihem mirë.** [nuk ndíhɛm mírə]
Call an ambulance!	**Thërrisni një ambulancë!** [θərísni ɲə ambulántsə!]
May I make a call?	**Mund të bëj një telefonatë?** [mund tə bəj ɲə tɛlɛfonátə?]

I'm sorry.	**Më vjen keq.** [mə vjɛn kɛc]
You're welcome.	**Ju lutem.** [ju lútɛm]

I, me	**unë, mua** [únə], [múa]
you (inform.)	**ti** [ti]
he	**ai** [ai]
she	**ajo** [ajó]
they (masc.)	**ata** [atá]
they (fem.)	**ato** [ató]
we	**ne** [nɛ]
you (pl)	**ju** [ju]
you (sg, form.)	**ju** [ju]

ENTRANCE	**HYRJE** [hýrjɛ]
EXIT	**DALJE** [dáljɛ]
OUT OF ORDER	**NUK FUNKSIONON** [nuk funksionón]
CLOSED	**MBYLLUR** [mbýɫur]

OPEN	**HAPUR** [hápur]
FOR WOMEN	**PËR FEMRA** [pər fémra]
FOR MEN	**PËR MESHKUJ** [pər méʃkuj]

Questions

Where?	**Ku?** [ku?]
Where to?	**Për ku?** [pər ku?]
Where from?	**Nga ku?** [ŋa ku?]
Why?	**Pse?** [psɛ?]
For what reason?	**Për çfarë arsye?** [pər tʃfárə arsýɛ?]
When?	**Kur?** [kur?]

How long?	**Sa kohë?** [sa kóhə?]
At what time?	**Në çfarë ore?** [nə tʃfárə órɛ?]
How much?	**Sa kushton?** [sa kuʃtón?]
Do you have ...?	**Keni ...?** [kéni ...?]
Where is ...?	**Ku ndodhet ...?** [ku ndóðɛt ...?]

What time is it?	**Sa është ora?** [sa əʃtə óra?]
May I make a call?	**Mund të bëj një telefonatë?** [mund tə bəj ɲə tɛlɛfonátə?]
Who's there?	**Kush është?** [kuʃ əʃtə?]
Can I smoke here?	**Mund të pi duhan këtu?** [mund tə pi duhán kətú?]
May I ...?	**Mund të ...?** [mund tə ...?]

Needs

I'd like ...	**Do të doja ...** [do tə dója ...]
I don't want ...	**Nuk dua ...** [nuk dúa ...]
I'm thirsty.	**Kam etje.** [kam étjɛ]
I want to sleep.	**Dua të fle.** [dúa tə flé]

I want ...	**Dua ...** [dúa ...]
to wash up	**të lahem** [tə láhɛm]
to brush my teeth	**të laj dhëmbët** [tə laj ðə́mbət]
to rest a while	**të pushoj pak** [tə puʃój pak]
to change my clothes	**të ndërrohem** [tə ndəróhɛm]

to go back to the hotel	**të kthehem në hotel** [tə kθéhɛm nə hotél]
to buy ...	**të blej ...** [tə blɛj ...]
to go to ...	**të shkoj në ...** [tə ʃkoj nə ...]
to visit ...	**të vizitoj ...** [tə vizitój ...]
to meet with ...	**të takohem me ...** [tə takóhɛm mɛ ...]
to make a call	**të bëj një telefonatë** [tə bəj ɲə tɛlɛfonátə]

I'm tired.	**Jam i /e/ lodhur.** [jam i /ɛ/ lóður]
We are tired.	**Jemi të lodhur.** [jémi tə lóður]
I'm cold.	**Kam ftohtë.** [kam ftóhtə]
I'm hot.	**Kam vapë.** [kam vápə]
I'm OK.	**Jam mirë.** [jam mirə]

I need to make a call.

Duhet të bëj një telefonatë.
[dúhɛt tə bəj ɲə tɛlɛfonátə]

I need to go to the restroom.

Duhet të shkoj në tualet.
[dúhɛt tə ʃkoj nə tualét]

I have to go.

Duhet të ik.
[dúhɛt tə ik]

I have to go now.

Duhet të ik tani.
[dúhɛt tə ik taní]

Asking for directions

Excuse me, ...	**Më falni, ...**
	[mə fálni, ...]
Where is ...?	**Ku ndodhet ...?**
	[ku ndóðɛt ...?]
Which way is ...?	**Si shkohet në ...?**
	[si ʃkóhɛt nə ...?]
Could you help me, please?	**Ju lutem, mund të më ndihmoni?**
	[ju lútɛm], [mund tə mə ndihmóni?]

I'm looking for ...	**Kërkoj ...**
	[kərkój ...]
I'm looking for the exit.	**Kërkoj daljen.**
	[kərkój dáljɛn]
I'm going to ...	**Po shkoj në ...**
	[po ʃkoj nə ...]
Am I going the right way to ...?	**A po shkoj siç duhet për në ...?**
	[a po ʃkoj sitʃ dúhɛt pər nə ...?]

Is it far?	**Është larg?**
	[əʃtə larg?]
Can I get there on foot?	**Mund të shkoj me këmbë deri atje?**
	[mund tə ʃkoj mɛ kə́mbə déri atjé?]
Can you show me on the map?	**Mund të më tregoni në hartë?**
	[mund tə mə trɛgóni nə hártə?]
Show me where we are right now.	**Më tregoni ku ndodhemi tani.**
	[mə trɛgóni ku ndóðɛmi taní]

Here	**Këtu**
	[kətú]
There	**Atje**
	[atjé]
This way	**Këtej**
	[kətéj]

Turn right.	**Kthehuni djathtas.**
	[kθéhuni djáθtas]
Turn left.	**Kthehuni majtas.**
	[kθéhuni májtas]
first (second, third) turn	**kthesa e parë (e dytë, e tretë)**
	[kθésa ɛ párə (ɛ dýtə), [ɛ trétə)]
to the right	**djathtas**
	[djáθtas]

to the left	**majtas** [májtas]
Go straight ahead.	**ecni drejt** [étsni dréjt]

Signs

WELCOME!	**MIRË SE ERDHËT!** [mírə sɛ érðət!]
ENTRANCE	**HYRJE** [hýrjɛ]
EXIT	**DALJE** [dáljɛ]

PUSH	**SHTY** [ʃty]
PULL	**TËRHIQ** [tərhíc]
OPEN	**HAPUR** [hápuɾ]
CLOSED	**MBYLLUR** [mbýɫuɾ]

FOR WOMEN	**PËR FEMRA** [pər fémra]
FOR MEN	**PËR MESHKUJ** [pər méʃkuj]
GENTLEMEN, GENTS	**ZOTËRINJ** [zotəriɲ]
WOMEN	**ZONJA** [zóɲa]

DISCOUNTS	**ULJE** [úljɛ]
SALE	**ULJE** [úljɛ]
FREE	**FALAS** [fálas]
NEW!	**E RE!** [ɛ ré!]
ATTENTION!	**KUJDES!** [kujdés!]

NO VACANCIES	**NUK KA VENDE TË LIRA** [nuk ka véndɛ tə líra]
RESERVED	**REZERVUAR** [rɛzɛrvúar]
ADMINISTRATION	**ADMINISTRATA** [administráta]
STAFF ONLY	**VETËM PËR PERSONELIN** [vétəm pər pɛrsonélin]

BEWARE OF THE DOG!	**KUJDES NGA QENI!** [kujdés ŋa céni!]
NO SMOKING!	**NDALOHET DUHANI!** [ndalóhɛt duháni!]
DO NOT TOUCH!	**MOS PREKNI!** [mos prékni!]
DANGEROUS	**I RREZIKSHËM** [i rɛzíkʃəm]
DANGER	**RREZIK** [rɛzík]
HIGH VOLTAGE	**VOLTAZH I LARTË** [voltáʒ i lártə]
NO SWIMMING!	**NDALOHET NOTI!** [ndalóhɛt nóti!]

OUT OF ORDER	**NUK FUNKSIONON** [nuk funksionón]
FLAMMABLE	**I DJEGSHËM** [i djégʃəm]
FORBIDDEN	**I NDALUAR** [i ndalúar]
NO TRESPASSING!	**NDALOHET KALIMI!** [ndalóhɛt kalími!]
WET PAINT	**BOJË E FRESKËT** [bójə ɛ fréskət]

CLOSED FOR RENOVATIONS	**MBYLLUR PËR RESTAURIM** [mbýɫur pər rɛstaurim]
WORKS AHEAD	**PO KRYHEN PUNIME** [po krýhɛn punímɛ]
DETOUR	**DEVIJIM** [dɛvijím]

Transportation. General phrases

plane	**avion** [avión]
train	**tren** [trɛn]
bus	**autobus** [autobús]
ferry	**traget** [tragét]
taxi	**taksi** [táksi]
car	**makinë** [makínə]

schedule	**orar** [orár]
Where can I see the schedule?	**Ku mund të shikoj oraret?** [ku mund tə ʃikój orárɛt?]
workdays (weekdays)	**ditë pune** [dítə púnɛ]
weekends	**fundjava** [fundjáva]
holidays	**pushime** [puʃímɛ]

DEPARTURE	**NISJE** [nísjɛ]
ARRIVAL	**MBËRRITJE** [mbəritjɛ]
DELAYED	**VONESË** [vonésə]
CANCELLED	**ANULUAR** [anulúar]

next (train, etc.)	**tjetër** [tjétər]
first	**parë** [párə]
last	**fundit** [fúndit]

When is the next ...?	**Kur është ... tjetër?** [kur əʃtə ... tjétər?]
When is the first ...?	**Kur është ... i parë?** [kur əʃtə ... i párə?]

When is the last ...?

Kur është ... i fundit?
[kur éʃtə ... i fúndit?]

transfer (change of trains, etc.)

ndërrim
[ndərím]

to make a transfer

të ndërroj
[tə ndərój]

Do I need to make a transfer?

Duhet të ndërroj?
[dúhɛt tə ndərój?]

Buying tickets

Where can I buy tickets?	**Ku mund të blej bileta?** [ku mund tə bléj biléta?]
ticket	**biletë** [bilétə]
to buy a ticket	**të blej biletë** [tə blɛj bilétə]
ticket price	**çmimi i biletës** [tʃmími i bilétəs]

Where to?	**Për ku?** [pər ku?]
To what station?	**Në cilin stacion?** [nə tsílin statsión?]
I need ...	**Më nevojitet ...** [mə nɛvojitɛt ...]
one ticket	**një biletë** [ɲə bilétə]
two tickets	**dy bileta** [dy biléta]
three tickets	**tre bileta** [trɛ biléta]

one-way	**vajtje** [vájtjɛ]
round-trip	**me kthim** [mɛ kθim]
first class	**klasi i parë** [klási i párə]
second class	**klasi i dytë** [klási i dýtə]

today	**sot** [sot]
tomorrow	**nesër** [nésər]
the day after tomorrow	**pasnesër** [pasnésər]
in the morning	**në mëngjes** [nə mənɟés]
in the afternoon	**në pasdite** [nə pasdítɛ]
in the evening	**në mbrëmje** [nə mbrə́mjɛ]

aisle seat

ulëse në korridor
[úləsɛ nə koridór]

window seat

ulëse tek dritarja
[úləsɛ tɛk dritárja]

How much?

Sa kushton?
[sa kuʃtón?]

Can I pay by credit card?

Mund të paguaj me kartelë krediti?
[mund tə pagúaj mɛ kartélə krɛdíti?]

Bus

bus	**autobus** [autobús]
intercity bus	**autobus urban** [autobús urbán]
bus stop	**stacion autobusi** [statsión autobúsi]
Where's the nearest bus stop?	**Ku ndodhet stacioni më i afërt i autobusit?** [ku ndóðɛt statsióni mə i áfərt i autobúsit?]
number (bus ~, etc.)	**numri** [númri]
Which bus do I take to get to ...?	**Cilin autobus duhet të marr për të shkuar në ...?** [tsílin autobús dúhɛt tə mar pər tə ʃkúar nə ...?]
Does this bus go to ...?	**A shkon ky autobus në ...?** [a ʃkon ky autobús nə ...?]
How frequent are the buses?	**Sa shpesh kalojnë autobusët?** [sa ʃpɛʃ kalójnə autobúsət?]
every 15 minutes	**çdo 15 minuta** [tʃdo pɛsəmbəðjétə minúta]
every half hour	**çdo gjysmë ore** [tʃdo ɟýsmə órɛ]
every hour	**çdo një orë** [tʃdo ɲə órə]
several times a day	**disa herë në ditë** [dísa hérə nə dítə]
... times a day	**... herë në ditë** [... hérə nə dítə]
schedule	**orari** [orári]
Where can I see the schedule?	**Ku mund të shikoj oraret?** [ku mund tə ʃikój orárɛt?]
When is the next bus?	**Kur është autobusi tjetër?** [kur ə́ʃtə autobúsi tjétər?]
When is the first bus?	**Kur është autobusi i parë?** [kur ə́ʃtə autobúsi i párə?]
When is the last bus?	**Kur është autobusi i fundit?** [kur ə́ʃtə autobúsi i fúndit?]

stop

stacion
[statsión]

next stop

stacioni tjetër
[statsióni tjétər]

last stop (terminus)

stacioni i fundit
[statsióni i fúndit]

Stop here, please.

Ju lutem, ndaloni këtu.
[ju lútɛm], [ndalóni kətú]

Excuse me, this is my stop.

Më falni, ky është stacioni im.
[mə fálni], [ky ə́ʃtə statsióni im]

Train

train	**tren** [trɛn]
suburban train	**tren lokal** [trɛn lokál]
long-distance train	**tren** [trɛn]
train station	**stacion treni** [statsión trɛni]
Excuse me, where is the exit to the platform?	**Më falni, ku është dalja për në platformë?** [mə fálni], [ku ə́ʃtə dálja pər nə platfórmə?]

Does this train go to ...?	**A shkon ky tren në ...?** [a ʃkon ky trɛn nə ...?]
next train	**treni tjetër** [tréni tjétər]
When is the next train?	**Kur vjen treni tjetër?** [kur vjɛn tréni tjétər?]
Where can I see the schedule?	**Ku mund të shikoj oraret?** [ku mund tə ʃikój orárɛt?]
From which platform?	**Nga cila platformë?** [ŋa tsíla platfórmə?]
When does the train arrive in ...?	**Kur arrin treni në ...** [kur arín tréni nə ...]

Please help me.	**Ju lutem më ndihmoni.** [ju lútɛm mə ndihmóni]
I'm looking for my seat.	**Kërkoj ulësen time.** [kərkój úləsɛn tímɛ]
We're looking for our seats.	**Po kërkojmë ulëset tona.** [po kərkójmə úləsɛt tóna]
My seat is taken.	**ulësja ime është zënë.** [úləsja ímɛ ə́ʃtə zə́nə]
Our seats are taken.	**ulëset tona janë zënë.** [úləsɛt tóna jánə zə́nə]

I'm sorry but this is my seat.	**Më falni por kjo është ulësja ime.** [mə fálni por kjo ə́ʃtə úləsja ímɛ]
Is this seat taken?	**A është e zënë kjo ulëse?** [a ə́ʃtə ɛ zə́nə kjo úləsɛ?]
May I sit here?	**Mund të ulem këtu?** [mund tə úlɛm kətú?]

On the train. Dialogue (No ticket)

Ticket, please.

Biletën, ju lutem.
[bilétən], [ju lútɛm]

I don't have a ticket.

Nuk kam biletë.
[nuk kam bilétə]

I lost my ticket.

Humba biletën.
[húmba bilétən]

I forgot my ticket at home.

E harrova biletën në shtëpi.
[ɛ haróva bilétən nə ʃtəpí]

You can buy a ticket from me.

Mund të blini biletën tek unë.
[mund tə blíni bilétən tɛk únə]

You will also have to pay a fine.

Duhet gjithashtu të paguani gjobë.
[dúhɛt ɟiθaʃtú tə pagúani ɟóbə]

Okay.

Në rregull.
[nə réguɫ]

Where are you going?

Ku po shkoni?
[ku po ʃkóni?]

I'm going to ...

Po shkoj në ...
[po ʃkoj nə ...]

How much? I don't understand.

Sa kushton? Nuk kuptoj.
[sa kuʃtón? nuk kuptój]

Write it down, please.

Shkruajeni, ju lutem.
[ʃkrúajɛni], [ju lútɛm]

Okay. Can I pay with a credit card?

Në rregull. Mund të paguaj me kartelë krediti?
[nə réguɫ. mund tə pagúaj mɛ kartélə krɛdíti?]

Yes, you can.

Po, mundeni.
[po], [múndɛni]

Here's your receipt.

Urdhëroni faturën.
[urðəróni fatúrən]

Sorry about the fine.

Më vjen keq për gjobën.
[mə vjɛn kɛc pər ɟóbən]

That's okay. It was my fault.

S'ka gjë. ishte gabimi im.
[s'ka ɟə. íʃtɛ gabími im]

Enjoy your trip.

Rrugë të mbarë.
[rúgə tə mbárə]

Taxi

taxi	**taksi** [táksi]
taxi driver	**shofer taksie** [ʃofér taksiɛ]
to catch a taxi	**të kap taksi** [tə kap táksi]
taxi stand	**stacion për taksi** [statsión pər táksi]
Where can I get a taxi?	**Ku mund të gjej një taksi?** [ku mund tə ɟɛj ɲə táksi?]
to call a taxi	**thërras një taksi** [θərás ɲə táksi]
I need a taxi.	**Më nevojitet taksi.** [mə nɛvojitɛt táksi]
Right now.	**Tani.** [taní]
What is your address (location)?	**Cila është adresa juaj?** [tsíla əʃtə adrésa júaj?]
My address is ...	**Adresa ime është ...** [adrésa imɛ əʃtə ...]
Your destination?	**Destinacioni juaj?** [dɛstinatsióni júaj?]
Excuse me, ...	**Më falni, ...** [mə fálni, ...]
Are you available?	**Jeni i lirë?** [jéni i lírə?]
How much is it to get to ...?	**Sa kushton deri në ...?** [sa kuʃtón déri nə ...?]
Do you know where it is?	**E dini ku ndodhet?** [ɛ dini ku ndóðɛt?]
Airport, please.	**Në aeroport, ju lutem.** [nə aɛropórt], [ju lútɛm]
Stop here, please.	**Ju lutem, ndaloni këtu.** [ju lútɛm], [ndalóni kətú]
It's not here.	**Nuk është këtu.** [nuk əʃtə kətú]
This is the wrong address.	**Kjo është adresë e gabuar.** [kjo əʃtə adrésə ɛ gabúar]
Turn left.	**Kthehuni majtas.** [kθéhuni májtas]
Turn right.	**Kthehuni djathtas.** [kθéhuni djáθtas]

How much do I owe you?

I'd like a receipt, please.

Keep the change.

Sa ju detyrohem?
[sa ju dɛtyróhɛm?]
Ju lutem, më jepni një faturë.
[ju lútɛm], [mə jépni ɲə fatúrə]
Mbajeni kusurin.
[mbájɛni kusúrin]

Would you please wait for me?

five minutes

ten minutes

fifteen minutes

twenty minutes

half an hour

Mund të më prisni, ju lutem?
[mund tə mə prísni], [ju lútɛm?]
pesë minuta
[pésə minúta]
dhjetë minuta
[ðjétə minúta]
pesëmbëdhjetë minuta
[pɛsəmbəðjétə minúta]
njëzet minuta
[ɲəzét minúta]
gjysmë ore
[ɟýsmə órɛ]

Hotel

Hello.	**Përshëndetje.** [pərʃəndétjɛ]
My name is …	**Më quajnë …** [mə cúajnə …]
I have a reservation.	**Kam një rezervim.** [kam ɲə rɛzɛrvím]
I need …	**Më nevojitet …** [mə nɛvojítɛt …]
a single room	**dhomë teke** [ðómə tékɛ]
a double room	**dhomë dyshe** [ðómə dýʃɛ]
How much is that?	**Sa kushton?** [sa kuʃtón?]
That's a bit expensive.	**Është pak shtrenjtë.** [éʃtə pak ʃtréɲtə]
Do you have anything else?	**Keni ndonjë gjë tjetër?** [kéni ndóɲə ɟə tjétər?]
I'll take it.	**Do ta marr.** [do ta mar]
I'll pay in cash.	**Do paguaj me para në dorë.** [do pagúaj mɛ pará nə dórə]
I've got a problem.	**Kam një problem.** [kam ɲə problém]
My … is broken.	**Më është prishur …** [mə éʃtə príʃur …]
My … is out of order.	**Nuk funksionon …** [nuk funksionón …]
TV	**televizor** [tɛlɛvizór]
air conditioner	**kondicioner** [konditsionér]
tap	**çezma** [tʃézma]
shower	**dushi** [duʃi]
sink	**lavamani** [lavamáni]
safe	**kasaforta** [kasafórta]

door lock	**brava e derës** [bráva ɛ dérəs]
electrical outlet	**paneli elektrik** [panéli ɛlɛktrík]
hairdryer	**tharësja e flokëve** [θárəsja ɛ flókɛvɛ]

I don't have ...	**Nuk kam ...** [nuk kam ...]
water	**ujë** [újə]
light	**drita** [dríta]
electricity	**korrent** [korént]

Can you give me ...?	**Mund të më jepni ...?** [mund tə mə jépni ...?]
a towel	**një peshqir** [ɲə pɛʃcir]
a blanket	**një çarçaf** [ɲə tʃartʃáf]
slippers	**shapka** [ʃápka]
a robe	**penuar** [pɛnuár]
shampoo	**shampo** [ʃampó]
soap	**sapun** [sapún]

I'd like to change rooms.	**Dua të ndryshoj dhomën.** [dúa tə ndryʃój ðómən]
I can't find my key.	**Nuk po gjej çelësin.** [nuk po ɟɛj tʃéləsin]
Could you open my room, please?	**Mund të më hapni derën, ju lutem?** [mund tə mə hápni dérən], [ju lútɛm?]
Who's there?	**Kush është?** [kuʃ əʃtə?]
Come in!	**Hyni!** [hýni!]
Just a minute!	**Një minutë!** [ɲə minútə!]
Not right now, please.	**Jo tani, ju lutem.** [jo taní], [ju lútɛm]

Come to my room, please.	**Ju lutem, ejani në dhomë.** [ju lútɛm], [éjani nə ðómə]
I'd like to order food service.	**Dua të porosisja ushqim.** [dúa tə porosísja uʃcím]
My room number is ...	**Numri i dhomës është ...** [númri i ðóməs əʃtə ...]

I'm leaving …	**Po largohem …** [po largóhɛm …]
We're leaving …	**Po largohemi …** [po largóhɛmi …]
right now	**tani** [taní]
this afternoon	**këtë pasdite** [kə́tə pasdítɛ]
tonight	**sonte** [sóntɛ]
tomorrow	**nesër** [nésər]
tomorrow morning	**nesër në mëngjes** [nésər nə mənɟés]
tomorrow evening	**nesër në mbrëmje** [nésər nə mbrə́mjɛ]
the day after tomorrow	**pasnesër** [pasnésər]

I'd like to pay.	**Dua të paguaj.** [dúa tə pagúaj]
Everything was wonderful.	**Gjithçka ishte e mrekullueshme.** [ɟiθtʃká iʃtɛ ɛ mrɛkuɫúɛʃmɛ]
Where can I get a taxi?	**Ku mund të gjej një taksi?** [ku mund tə ɟɛj ɲə táksi?]
Would you call a taxi for me, please?	**Mund të më thërrisni një taksi, ju lutem?** [mund tə mə θərísni ɲə táksi], [ju lútɛm?]

Restaurant

Can I look at the menu, please?

Table for one.

There are two (three, four) of us.

Mund të shoh menynë, ju lutem?
[mund tə ʃoh mɛnýnə], [ju lútɛm?]

Tavolinë për një person.
[tavolínə pər ɲə pɛrsón]

Jemi dy (tre, katër) vetë.
[jémi dy (trɛ], [kátər) vétə]

Smoking

No smoking

Excuse me! (addressing a waiter)

menu

wine list

The menu, please.

Lejohet duhani
[lɛjóhɛt duháni]

Ndalohet duhani
[ndalóhɛt duháni]

Më falni!
[mə fálni!]

menyja
[mɛnýja]

menyja e verave
[mɛnýja ɛ véravɛ]

Menynë, ju lutem.
[mɛnýnə], [ju lútɛm]

Are you ready to order?

What will you have?

I'll have …

Jeni gati për të dhënë porosinë?
[jéni gáti pər tə ðənə porosínə?]

Çfarë do të merrni?
[tʃfárə do tə mérni?]

Do të marr …
[do tə mar …]

I'm a vegetarian.

meat

fish

vegetables

Do you have vegetarian dishes?

I don't eat pork.

Band-Aid

I am allergic to …

Jam vegjetarian /vegjetariane/.
[jam vɛɟɛtarián /vɛɟɛtariánɛ/]

mish
[miʃ]

peshk
[pɛʃk]

perime
[pɛrímɛ]

Keni gatime për vegjetarianë?
[kéni gatímɛ pər vɛɟɛtariánə?]

Nuk ha mish derri.
[nuk ha miʃ déri]

Ai /Ajo/ nuk ha mish.
[aí /ajó/ nuk ha miʃ]

Kam alergji nga …
[kam alɛɟí ŋa …]

Would you please bring me … | **Mund të më sillni …**
[mund tə mə siłni …]

salt | pepper | sugar | **kripë | piper | sheqer**
[krípə | pipér | ʃɛcér]

coffee | tea | dessert | **kafe | çaj | ëmbëlsirë**
[káfɛ | tʃaj | əmbəlsírə]

water | sparkling | plain | **ujë | me gaz | pa gaz**
[újə | mɛ gaz | pa gaz]

a spoon | fork | knife | **një lugë | pirun | thikë**
[ɲə lúgə | pirún | θíkə]

a plate | napkin | **një pjatë | pecetë**
[ɲə pjátə | pɛtsétə]

Enjoy your meal! | **Ju bëftë mirë!**
[ju bə́ftə mírə!]

One more, please. | **Dhe një tjetër, ju lutem.**
[ðɛ ɲə tjétər], [ju lútɛm]

It was very delicious. | **ishte shumë e shijshme.**
[iʃtɛ ʃúmə ɛ ʃijʃmɛ]

check | change | tip | **llogari | kusur | bakshish**
[łogarí | kusúr | bakʃíʃ]

Check, please.
(Could I have the check, please?) | **Llogarinë, ju lutem.**
[łogarínə], [ju lútɛm]

Can I pay by credit card? | **Mund të paguaj me kartelë krediti?**
[mund tə pagúaj mɛ kartélə krɛdíti?]

I'm sorry, there's a mistake here. | **Më falni por ka një gabim këtu.**
[mə fálni por ka ɲə gabím kətú]

Shopping

Can I help you?	**Mund t'ju ndihmoj?** [mund t'ju ndihmój?]
Do you have ...?	**Keni ...?** [kéni ...?]
I'm looking for ...	**Kërkoj ...** [kərkój ...]
I need ...	**Më nevojitet ...** [mə nɛvojítɛt ...]

I'm just looking.	**Thjesht po shoh.** [θjɛʃt po ʃoh]
We're just looking.	**Thjesht po shohim.** [θjɛʃt po ʃóhim]
I'll come back later.	**Do vij më vonë.** [do víj mə vónə]
We'll come back later.	**Do vijmë më vonë.** [do víjmə mə vónə]
discounts	sale	**ulje çmimesh	ulje** [úljɛ tʃmímɛʃ	úljɛ]

Would you please show me ...	**Ju lutem mund të më tregoni ...** [ju lútɛm mund tə mə trɛgóni ...]
Would you please give me ...	**Ju lutem mund të më jepni ...** [ju lútɛm mund tə mə jépni ...]
Can I try it on?	**Mund ta provoj?** [mund ta provój?]
Excuse me, where's the fitting room?	**Më falni, ku është dhoma e provës?** [mə fálni], [ku əʃtə ðóma ɛ próvəs?]
Which color would you like?	**Çfarë ngjyre e doni?** [tʃfárə njýrɛ ɛ dóni?]
size	length	**numri	gjatësia** [númri	jatəsía]
How does it fit?	**Si ju rri?** [si ju ri?]

How much is it?	**Sa kushton?** [sa kuʃtón?]
That's too expensive.	**Është shumë shtrenjtë.** [əʃtə ʃúmə ʃtréɲtə]
I'll take it.	**Do ta marr.** [do ta mar]
Excuse me, where do I pay?	**Më falni, ku duhet të paguaj?** [mə fálni], [ku dúhɛt tə pagúaj?]

Will you pay in cash or credit card?

Do paguani me para në dorë apo kartelë krediti?
[do pagúani mɛ pará nə dórə apo kartélə krɛdíti?]

In cash | with credit card

Me para në dorë | me kartelë krediti
[mɛ pará nə dórə | mɛ kartélə krɛdíti]

Do you want the receipt?

Dëshironi faturën?
[dəʃiróni fatúrən?]

Yes, please.

Po faleminderit.
[po falɛmindérit]

No, it's OK.

Jo, s'ka problem.
[jo], [s'ka problém]

Thank you. Have a nice day!

Faleminderit. Ditë të mbarë!
[falɛmindérit. dítə tə mbárə!]

In town

Excuse me, ...	**Më falni, ju lutem.** [mə fálni], [ju lútɛm]
I'm looking for ...	**Kërkoj ...** [kərkój ...]
the subway	**metronë** [mɛtrónə]
my hotel	**hotelin** [hotélin]
the movie theater	**kinemanë** [kinɛmánə]
a taxi stand	**një stacion për taksi** [ɲə statsión pər táksi]

an ATM	**një bankomat** [ɲə bankomát]
a foreign exchange office	**një zyrë shkëmbimi parash** [ɲə zýrə ʃkəmbími paráʃ]
an internet café	**një internet kafe** [ɲə intɛrnét káfɛ]
... street	**rrugën ...** [rúgən ...]
this place	**këtë vend** [kə́tə vɛnd]

Do you know where ... is?	**Dini ku ndodhet ...?** [díni ku ndóðɛt ...?]
Which street is this?	**Cila rrugë është kjo?** [tsíla rúgə ə́ʃtə kjó?]
Show me where we are right now.	**Më tregoni ku ndodhemi tani.** [mə trɛgóni ku ndóðɛmi taní]
Can I get there on foot?	**Mund të shkoj me këmbë deri atje?** [mund tə ʃkoj mɛ kə́mbə déri atjé?]
Do you have a map of the city?	**Keni hartë të qytetit?** [kéni hártə tə cytétit?]

How much is a ticket to get in?	**Sa kushton një biletë hyrje?** [sa kuʃtón ɲə bilétə hýrjɛ?]
Can I take pictures here?	**Mund të bëj fotografi këtu?** [mund tə bəj fotografí kətú?]
Are you open?	**Jeni të hapur?** [jéni tə hápur?]

When do you open? **Kur hapeni?**
[kur hápɛni?]

When do you close? **Kur mbylleni?**
[kur mbýłɛni?]

Money

money	**para** [pará]
cash	**para në dorë** [pará nə dórə]
paper money	**kartëmonedha** [kartəmonéða]
loose change	**kusur** [kusúr]
check | change | tip	**llogari | kusur | bakshish** [łogarí | kusúr | bakʃíʃ]

credit card	**kartelë krediti** [kartélə krɛdíti]
wallet	**portofol** [portofól]
to buy	**të blej** [tə blɛj]
to pay	**të paguaj** [tə pagúaj]
fine	**gjobë** [ɟóbə]
free	**falas** [fálas]

Where can I buy ...?	**Ku mund të blej ...?** [ku mund tə bléj ...?]
Is the bank open now?	**Është banka e hapur tani?** [éʃtə bánka ɛ hápur taní?]
When does it open?	**Kur hapet?** [kur hápɛt?]
When does it close?	**Kur mbyllet?** [kur mbýłɛt?]

How much?	**Sa kushton?** [sa kuʃtón?]
How much is this?	**Sa kushton kjo?** [sa kuʃtón kjo?]
That's too expensive.	**Është shumë shtrenjtë.** [éʃtə ʃúmə ʃtréɲtə]

Excuse me, where do I pay?	**Më falni, ku duhet të paguaj?** [mə fálni], [ku dúhɛt tə pagúaj?]
Check, please.	**Llogarinë, ju lutem.** [łogarínə], [ju lútɛm]

Can I pay by credit card?

Mund të paguaj me kartelë krediti?
[mund tə pagúaj mɛ kartélə krɛdíti?]

Is there an ATM here?

Ka ndonjë bankomat këtu?
[ka ndónə bankomát kətú?]

I'm looking for an ATM.

Kërkoj një bankomat.
[kərkój ɲə bankomát]

I'm looking for a foreign exchange office.

Kërkoj një zyrë të këmbimit valutor.
[kərkój ɲə zýrə tə kəmbímit valutór]

I'd like to change ...

Dua të këmbej ...
[dúa tə kəmbéj ...]

What is the exchange rate?

Sa është kursi i këmbimit?
[sa ə́ʃtə kúrsi i kəmbímit?]

Do you need my passport?

Ju duhet pasaporta ime?
[ju dúhɛt pasapórta imɛ?]

Time

What time is it?	**Sa është ora?** [sa ə́ʃtə óra?]
When?	**Kur?** [kur?]
At what time?	**Në çfarë ore?** [nə tʃfárə órɛ?]
now | later | after ...	**tani | më vonë | pas ...** [taní | mə vónə | pas ...]

one o'clock	**ora një** [óra ɲə]
one fifteen	**një e çerek** [ɲə ɛ tʃɛrék]
one thirty	**një e tridhjetë** [ɲə ɛ triðjétə]
one forty-five	**një e dyzet e pesë** [ɲə ɛ dyzét ɛ pésə]

one | two | three	**një | dy | tre** [ɲə | dy | trɛ]
four | five | six	**katër | pesë | gjashtë** [kátər | pésə | ɟáʃtə]
seven | eight | nine	**shtatë | tetë | nëntë** [ʃtátə | tétə | néntə]
ten | eleven | twelve	**dhjetë | njëmbëdhjetë | dymbëdhjetë** [ðjétə | ɲəmbəðjétə | dymbəðjétə]

in ...	**për ...** [pər ...]
five minutes	**pesë minuta** [pésə minúta]
ten minutes	**dhjetë minuta** [ðjétə minúta]
fifteen minutes	**pesëmbëdhjetë minuta** [pɛsəmbəðjétə minúta]
twenty minutes	**njëzet minuta** [ɲəzét minúta]
half an hour	**gjysmë ore** [ɟýsmə órɛ]
an hour	**një orë** [ɲə órə]

in the morning	**në mëngjes** [nə mənɟés]
early in the morning	**në mëngjes herët** [nə mənɟés hérət]
this morning	**sot në mëngjes** [sot nə mənɟés]
tomorrow morning	**nesër në mëngjes** [nésər nə mənɟés]
in the middle of the day	**në mesditë** [nə mɛsdítə]
in the afternoon	**në pasdite** [nə pasdítɛ]
in the evening	**në mbrëmje** [nə mbrəmjɛ]
tonight	**sonte** [sóntɛ]
at night	**natën** [nátən]
yesterday	**dje** [djé]
today	**sot** [sot]
tomorrow	**nesër** [nésər]
the day after tomorrow	**pasnesër** [pasnésər]
What day is it today?	**Çfarë dite është sot?** [tʃfárə dítɛ əʃtə sot?]
It's ...	**Është ...** [əʃtə ...]
Monday	**E hënë** [ɛ hə́nə]
Tuesday	**E martë** [ɛ mártə]
Wednesday	**E mërkurë** [ɛ mərkúrə]
Thursday	**E enjte** [ɛ éɲtɛ]
Friday	**E premte** [ɛ prémtɛ]
Saturday	**E shtunë** [ɛ ʃtúnə]
Sunday	**E diel** [ɛ díɛl]

Greetings. Introductions

Hello. **Përshëndetje.**
[pərʃəndétjɛ]

Pleased to meet you. **Kënaqësi që u njohëm.**
[kənacəsí cə u ɲóhəm]

Me too. **Gjithashtu.**
[ɟiθaʃtú]

I'd like you to meet ... **Ju prezantoj me ...**
[ju prɛzantój mɛ ...]

Nice to meet you. **Gëzohem që u njohëm.**
[gəzóhɛm cə u ɲóhəm]

How are you? **Si jeni?**
[si jéni?]

My name is ... **Më quajnë ...**
[mə cúajnə ...]

His name is ... **Ai quhet ...**
[ai cúhɛt ...]

Her name is ... **Ajo quhet ...**
[ajó cúhɛt ...]

What's your name? **Si quheni?**
[si cúhɛni?]

What's his name? **Si e quajnë?**
[si ɛ cúajnə?]

What's her name? **Si e quajnë?**
[si ɛ cúajnə?]

What's your last name? **Si e keni mbiemrin?**
[si ɛ kéni mbiémrin?]

You can call me ... **Mund të më thërrisni ...**
[mund tə mə θərísni ...]

Where are you from? **Nga jeni?**
[ŋa jéni?]

I'm from ... **Jam nga ...**
[jam ŋa ...]

What do you do for a living? **Me çfarë merreni?**
[mɛ tʃfárə mérɛni?]

Who is this? **Kush është ky?**
[kuʃ əʃtə ky?]

Who is he? **Kush është ai?**
[kuʃ əʃtə ái?]

Who is she?	**Kush është ajo?**
	[kuʃ əʃtə ajó?]
Who are they?	**Kush janë ata?**
	[kuʃ jánə atá?]

This is ...	**Ky /Kjo/ është ...**
	[ky /kjo/ əʃtə ...]
my friend (masc.)	**shoku im**
	[ʃóku im]
my friend (fem.)	**shoqja ime**
	[ʃócja ímɛ]
my husband	**bashkëshorti im**
	[baʃkəʃórti im]
my wife	**bashkëshortja ime**
	[baʃkəʃórtja imɛ]

my father	**babai im**
	[babái im]
my mother	**nëna ime**
	[nə́na ímɛ]
my brother	**vëllai im**
	[vəɫái im]
my sister	**motra ime**
	[mótra imɛ]
my son	**djali im**
	[djáli im]
my daughter	**vajza ime**
	[vájza imɛ]

This is our son.	**Ky është djali ynë.**
	[ky əʃtə djáli ýnə]
This is our daughter.	**Kjo është vajza jonë.**
	[kjo əʃtə vájza jónə]
These are my children.	**Këta janë fëmijët e mi.**
	[kətá jánə fəmíjət ɛ mi]
These are our children.	**Këta janë fëmijët tanë.**
	[kətá jánə fəmíjət tánə]

Farewells

Good bye!	**Mirupafshim!** [mirupáfʃim!]
Bye! (inform.)	**Pafshim!** [páfʃim!]
See you tomorrow.	**Shihemi nesër.** [ʃíhɛmi nésər]
See you soon.	**Shihemi së shpejti.** [ʃíhɛmi sə ʃpéjti]
See you at seven.	**Shihemi në orën shtatë.** [ʃíhɛmi nə órən ʃtátə]
Have fun!	**ia kalofshi mirë!** [ía kalófʃi mírə!]
Talk to you later.	**Flasim më vonë.** [flásim mə vónə]
Have a nice weekend.	**Fundjavë të këndshme.** [fundjávə tə kəndʃmɛ]
Good night.	**Natën e mirë.** [nátən ɛ mírə]
It's time for me to go.	**erdhi koha të ik.** [érði kóha tə ik]
I have to go.	**Duhet të ik.** [dúhɛt tə ik]
I will be right back.	**Kthehem menjëherë.** [kθéhɛm mɛɲəhérə]
It's late.	**Është vonë.** [əʃtə vónə]
I have to get up early.	**Duhet të ngrihem herët.** [dúhɛt tə ŋríhɛm hérət]
I'm leaving tomorrow.	**Do ik nesër.** [do ik nésər]
We're leaving tomorrow.	**Do ikim nesër.** [do íkim nésər]
Have a nice trip!	**Udhëtim të mbarë!** [uðətím tə mbárə!]
It was nice meeting you.	**ishte kënaqësi.** [íʃtɛ kənacəsí]
It was nice talking to you.	**ishte kënaqësi që folëm.** [íʃtɛ kənacəsí cə fóləm]
Thanks for everything.	**Faleminderit për gjithçka.** [falɛmindérit pər ɟíθtʃka]

I had a very good time.

ia kalova shumë mirë.
[ía kalóva ʃúmə mírə]

We had a very good time.

ia kaluam shumë mirë.
[ía kalúam ʃúmə mírə]

It was really great.

ishte vërtet fantastike.
[íʃtɛ vərtét fantastíkɛ]

I'm going to miss you.

Do më marrë malli.
[do mə márə máɫi]

We're going to miss you.

Do na marrë malli.
[do na márə máɫi]

Good luck!

Suksese!
[suksésɛ!]

Say hi to …

I bën të fala …
[i bən tə fála …]

Foreign language

I don't understand.	**Nuk kuptoj.** [nuk kuptój]
Write it down, please.	**Shkruajeni, ju lutem.** [ʃkrúajɛni], [ju lútɛm]
Do you speak ...?	**Flisni ...?** [flísni ...?]

I speak a little bit of ...	**Flas pak ...** [flás pak ...]
English	**Anglisht** [aŋlíʃt]
Turkish	**Turqisht** [turcíʃt]
Arabic	**Arabisht** [arabíʃt]
French	**Frëngjisht** [frənɟíʃt]

German	**Gjermanisht** [ɟɛrmaníʃt]
Italian	**Italisht** [italíʃt]
Spanish	**Spanjisht** [spaɲíʃt]
Portuguese	**Portugalisht** [portugalíʃt]
Chinese	**Kinezisht** [kinɛzíʃt]
Japanese	**Japonisht** [japoníʃt]

Can you repeat that, please.	**Mund ta përsërisni, ju lutem.** [mund ta pərsərísni], [ju lútɛm]
I understand.	**Kuptoj.** [kuptój]
I don't understand.	**Nuk kuptoj.** [nuk kuptój]
Please speak more slowly.	**Ju lutem, flisni më ngadalë.** [ju lútɛm], [flísni mə ŋadálə]

Is that correct? (Am I saying it right?)	**E saktë?** [ɛ sáktə?]
What is this? (What does this mean?)	**Çfarë është kjo?** [tʃfárə əʃtə kjó?]

Apologies

Excuse me, please.   **Më falni.**
                            [mə fálni]

I'm sorry.   **Më vjen keq.**
                            [mə vjɛn kɛc]

I'm really sorry.   **Më vjen shumë keq.**
                            [mə vjɛn ʃúmə kɛc]

Sorry, it's my fault.   **Më fal, është faji im.**
                            [mə fal], [ə́ʃtə fájí im]

My mistake.   **Gabimi im.**
                            [gabími im]

May I ...?   **Mund të ...?**
                            [mund tə ...?]

Do you mind if I ...?   **Ju vjen keq nëse ...?**
                            [ju vjɛn kɛc nə́sɛ ...?]

It's OK.   **Është në rregull.**
                            [ə́ʃtə nə régutʰ]

It's all right.   **Është në rregull.**
                            [ə́ʃtə nə régutʰ]

Don't worry about it.   **Mos u shqetësoni.**
                            [mos u ʃcɛtəsóni]

Agreement

Yes.	**Po.** [po]
Yes, sure.	**Po, sigurisht.** [po], [siguríʃt]
OK (Good!)	**Në rregull.** [nə réguɫ]
Very well.	**Shumë mirë.** [ʃúmə mírə]
Certainly!	**Sigurisht!** [siguríʃt!]
I agree.	**Jam dakord.** [jam dakórd]
That's correct.	**E saktë.** [ɛ sáktə]
That's right.	**E drejtë.** [ɛ dréjtə]
You're right.	**Keni të drejtë.** [kéni tə dréjtə]
I don't mind.	**S'e kam problem.** [s'ɛ kam problém]
Absolutely right.	**Absolutisht e drejtë.** [absolutíʃt ɛ dréjtə]
It's possible.	**Është e mundur.** [əʃtə ɛ múndur]
That's a good idea.	**Ide e mirë.** [idé ɛ mírə]
I can't say no.	**Nuk them dot jo.** [nuk θɛm dot jo]
I'd be happy to.	**Është kënaqësi.** [əʃtə kənacəsí]
With pleasure.	**Me kënaqësi.** [mɛ kənacəsí]

Refusal. Expressing doubt

No.	**Jo.** [jo]
Certainly not.	**Sigurisht që jo.** [siguriʃt cə jo]

I don't agree.	**Nuk jam dakord.** [nuk jam dakórd]
I don't think so.	**Nuk ma ha mendja.** [nuk ma ha méndja]
It's not true.	**Nuk është e vërtetë.** [nuk éʃtə ɛ vərtétə]

You are wrong.	**E keni gabim.** [ɛ kéni gabím]
I think you are wrong.	**Më duket se e keni gabim.** [mə dúkɛt sɛ ɛ kéni gabím]
I'm not sure.	**Nuk jam i sigurt.** [nuk jam i sígurt]
It's impossible.	**Është e pamundur.** [éʃtə ɛ pámundur]
Nothing of the kind (sort)!	**Asgjë e këtij lloji!** [asɟə ɛ kətíj tóji!]

The exact opposite.	**Krejt e kundërta.** [kréjt ɛ kúndərta]
I'm against it.	**Jam kundër.** [jam kúndər]
I don't care.	**Nuk më intereson.** [nuk mə intɛrɛsón]
I have no idea.	**Nuk e kam idenë.** [nuk ɛ kam idénə]
I doubt it.	**Dyshoj.** [dyʃój]

Sorry, I can't.	**Më falni, nuk mundem.** [mə fálni], [nuk múndɛm]
Sorry, I don't want to.	**Më vjen keq, nuk dua.** [mə vjɛn kɛc], [nuk dúa]
Thank you, but I don't need this.	**Faleminderit, por s'kam nevojë për këtë.** [falɛmindérit], [por s'kam nɛvójə pər kətə]

It's getting late.

Po shkon vonë.
[po ʃkon vónə]

I have to get up early.

Duhet të ngrihem herët.
[dúhɛt tə ŋríhɛm hérət]

I don't feel well.

Nuk ndihem mirë.
[nuk ndíhɛm mírə]

Expressing gratitude

Thank you.	**Faleminderit.**
	[falɛmindérit]
Thank you very much.	**Faleminderit shumë.**
	[falɛmindérit ʃúmə]
I really appreciate it.	**E vlerësoj shumë.**
	[ɛ vlɛrəsój ʃúmə]
I'm really grateful to you.	**Ju jam shumë mirënjohës.**
	[ju jam ʃúmə mirəɲóhəs]
We are really grateful to you.	**Ju jemi shumë mirënjohës.**
	[ju jémi ʃúmə mirəɲóhəs]
Thank you for your time.	**Faleminderit për kohën që më kushtuat.**
	[falɛmindérit pər kóhən cə mə kuʃtúat]
Thanks for everything.	**Faleminderit për gjithçka.**
	[falɛmindérit pər ɟíθtʃka]
Thank you for ...	**Faleminderit për ...**
	[falɛmindérit pər ...]
your help	**ndihmën tuaj**
	[ndíhmən túaj]
a nice time	**kohën e këndshme**
	[kóhən ɛ kéndʃmɛ]
a wonderful meal	**një vakt i mrekullueshëm**
	[ɲə vakt i mrɛkuɫúeʃəm]
a pleasant evening	**një mbrëmje e këndshme**
	[ɲə mbrémjɛ ɛ kéndʃmɛ]
a wonderful day	**një ditë e mrekullueshme**
	[ɲə dítə ɛ mrɛkuɫúeʃmɛ]
an amazing journey	**një udhëtim i mahnitshëm**
	[ɲə uðətím i mahnítʃəm]
Don't mention it.	**Mos u shqetësoni fare.**
	[mos u ʃcɛtəsóni fárɛ]
You are welcome.	**Ju lutem.**
	[ju lútɛm]
Any time.	**Në çdo kohë.**
	[nə tʃdo kóhə]
My pleasure.	**Kënaqësia ime.**
	[kənacəsía ímɛ]

Forget it.

Harroje.
[harójɛ]

Don't worry about it.

Mos u shqetësoni.
[mos u ʃcɛtəsóni]

Congratulations. Best wishes

Congratulations!	**Urime!**
	[urímɛ!]
Happy birthday!	**Gëzuar ditëlindjen!**
	[gəzúar ditəlíndjɛn!]
Merry Christmas!	**Gëzuar Krishtlindjet!**
	[gəzúar kriʃtlíndjɛt!]
Happy New Year!	**Gëzuar Vitin e Ri!**
	[gəzúar vitin ɛ ri!]
Happy Easter!	**Gëzuar Pashkët!**
	[gəzúar páʃkət!]
Happy Hanukkah!	**Gëzuar Hanukkah!**
	[gəzúar hanúkkah!]
I'd like to propose a toast.	**Dua të ngre një dolli.**
	[dúa tə ŋré ɲə doɫí]
Cheers!	**Gëzuar!**
	[gəzúar!]
Let's drink to …!	**Le të pijmë në shëndetin e …!**
	[lɛ tə pijmə nə ʃəndétin ɛ …!]
To our success!	**Për suksesin tonë!**
	[pər suksésin tónə!]
To your success!	**Për suksesin tuaj!**
	[pər suksésin túaj!]
Good luck!	**Suksese!**
	[suksésɛ!]
Have a nice day!	**Uroj një ditë të mbarë!**
	[urój ɲə dítə tə mbárə!]
Have a good holiday!	**Uroj pushime të këndshme!**
	[urój puʃímɛ tə kə́ndʃmɛ!]
Have a safe journey!	**Udhëtim të mbarë!**
	[uðətím tə mbárə!]
I hope you get better soon!	**Ju dëshiroj shërim të shpejtë!**
	[ju dəʃirój ʃərím tə ʃpéjtə!]

Socializing

Why are you sad?	**Pse jeni i /e/ mërzitur?** [psɛ jéni i /ɛ/ mərzítur?]
Smile! Cheer up!	**Buzëqeshni! Gëzohuni!** [buzəcéʃni! gəzóhuni!]
Are you free tonight?	**Je i /e/ lirë sonte?** [jɛ i /ɛ/ lírə sóntɛ?]

May I offer you a drink?	**Mund t'ju ofroj një pije?** [mund t'ju ofrój ɲə píjɛ?]
Would you like to dance?	**Doni të kërcejmë?** [dóni tə kərtséjmə?]
Let's go to the movies.	**Shkojmë në kinema.** [ʃkójmə nə kinɛmá]

May I invite you to …?	**Mund t'ju ftoj …?** [mund t'ju ftoj …?]
a restaurant	**në restorant** [nə rɛstoránt]
the movies	**në kinema** [nə kinɛmá]
the theater	**në teatër** [nə tɛátər]
go for a walk	**për një shëtitje** [pər ɲə ʃətítjɛ]

At what time?	**Në çfarë ore?** [nə tʃfárə órɛ?]
tonight	**sonte** [sóntɛ]
at six	**në gjashtë** [nə ɟáʃtə]
at seven	**në shtatë** [nə ʃtátə]
at eight	**në tetë** [nə tétə]
at nine	**në nëntë** [nə nəntə]

Do you like it here?	**Ju pëlqen këtu?** [ju pəlcén kətú?]
Are you here with someone?	**Keni ardhur të shoqëruar?** [kéni árður tə ʃocərúar?]
I'm with my friend.	**Jam me një shok /shoqe/.** [jam mɛ ɲə ʃok /ʃócɛ/]

I'm with my friends.

Jam me shoqëri.
[jam mɛ ʃocərí]

No, I'm alone.

Jo, jam vetëm.
[jo], [jam vétəm]

Do you have a boyfriend?

Ke të dashur?
[kɛ tə dáʃur?]

I have a boyfriend.

Kam të dashur.
[kam tə dáʃur]

Do you have a girlfriend?

Ke të dashur?
[kɛ tə dáʃur?]

I have a girlfriend.

Kam të dashur.
[kam tə dáʃur]

Can I see you again?

Mund të takohemi përsëri?
[mund tə takóhɛmi pərsəri?]

Can I call you?

Mund të të telefonoj?
[mund tə tə tɛlɛfonój?]

Call me. (Give me a call.)

Më telefono.
[mə tɛlɛfonó]

What's your number?

Cili është numri yt?
[tsíli əʃtə númri yt?]

I miss you.

Më mungon.
[mə muŋón]

You have a beautiful name.

Keni emër të bukur.
[kéni émər tə búkur]

I love you.

Të dua.
[tə dúa]

Will you marry me?

Do martohesh me mua?
[do martóheʃ mɛ múa?]

You're kidding!

Bëni shaka!
[bəni ʃaká!]

I'm just kidding.

Bëj shaka.
[bəj ʃaká]

Are you serious?

E keni seriozisht?
[ɛ kéni sɛriozíʃt?]

I'm serious.

E kam seriozisht.
[ɛ kam sɛriozíʃt]

Really?!

Vërtet?!
[vərtét?!]

It's unbelievable!

E pabesueshme!
[ɛ pabɛsúɛʃmɛ!]

I don't believe you.

S'ju besoj.
[s'ju bɛsój]

I can't.

S'mundem.
[s'múndɛm]

I don't know.

Nuk e di.
[nuk ɛ di]

I don't understand you.

Nuk ju kuptoj.
[nuk ju kuptój]

Please go away.

Leave me alone!

Ju lutem largohuni.
[ju lútɛm largóhuni]

Më lini të qetë!
[mə líni tə cétə!]

I can't stand him.

You are disgusting!

I'll call the police!

Se duroj dot.
[sɛ durój dot]

Jeni të neveritshëm!
[jéni tə nɛvɛrítʃəm!]

Do thërras policinë!
[do θərás politsínə!]

Sharing impressions. Emotions

I like it.	**Më pëlqen.** [mə pəlcén]
Very nice.	**Shumë bukur** [ʃúmə búkur]
That's great!	**Fantastike!** [fantastíkɛ!]
It's not bad.	**Nuk është keq.** [nuk əʃtə kɛc]

I don't like it.	**Nuk më pëlqen.** [nuk mə pəlcén]
It's not good.	**Nuk është mirë.** [nuk əʃtə mírə]
It's bad.	**Është keq.** [əʃtə kɛc]
It's very bad.	**Është shumë keq.** [əʃtə ʃúmə kɛc]
It's disgusting.	**Është e shpifur.** [əʃtə ɛ ʃpífur]

I'm happy.	**Jam i /e/ lumtur.** [jam i /ɛ/ lúmtur]
I'm content.	**Jam i /e/ kënaqur.** [jam i /ɛ/ kənácur]
I'm in love.	**Jam i /e/ dashuruar.** [jam i /ɛ/ daʃurúar]
I'm calm.	**Jam i /e/ qetë.** [jam i /ɛ/ cétə]
I'm bored.	**Jam i /e/ mërzitur.** [jam i /ɛ/ mərzitur]

I'm tired.	**Jam i /e/ lodhur.** [jam i /ɛ/ lóður]
I'm sad.	**Jam i /e/ trishtuar.** [jam i /ɛ/ triʃtúar]

I'm frightened.	**Jam i /e/ frikësuar.** [jam i /ɛ/ frikəsúar]
I'm angry.	**Jam i /e/ zemëruar.** [jam i /ɛ/ zɛmərúar]
I'm worried.	**Jam i /e/ shqetësuar.** [jam i /ɛ/ ʃcɛtəsúar]
I'm nervous.	**Jam nervoz /nervoze/.** [jam nɛrvóz /nɛrvózɛ/]

I'm jealous. (envious)

Jam xheloz /xheloze/.
[jam dʒɛlóz /dʒɛlózɛ/]

I'm surprised.

Jam i /e/ befasuar.
[jam i /ɛ/ bɛfasúar]

I'm perplexed.

Jam i /e/ hutuar.
[jam i /ɛ/ hutúar]

Problems. Accidents

I've got a problem.

Kam një problem.
[kam ɲə problém]

We've got a problem.

Kemi një problem.
[kémi ɲə problém]

I'm lost.

Kam humbur.
[kam húmbur]

I missed the last bus (train).

Humba autobusin e fundit.
[húmba autobúsin ɛ fúndit]

I don't have any money left.

Kam mbetur pa para.
[kam mbétur pa pará]

I've lost my ...

Humba ...
[húmba ...]

Someone stole my ...

Dikush më vodhi ...
[dikúʃ mə vóði ...]

passport

pasaportën
[pasapórtən]

wallet

portofol
[portofól]

papers

dokumentet
[dokuméntɛt]

ticket

biletën
[bilétən]

money

para
[pará]

handbag

çantën
[tʃántən]

camera

aparatin fotografik
[aparátin fotografík]

laptop

laptop
[laptóp]

tablet computer

kompjuterin tabletë
[kompjutérin tablétə]

mobile phone

celularin
[tsɛlulárin]

Help me!

Ndihmë!
[ndíhmə!]

What's happened?

Çfarë ndodhi?
[tʃfárə ndóði?]

fire

zjarr
[zjar]

shooting

të shtëna
[tə ʃténa]

murder	**vrasje** [vrásjɛ]
explosion	**shpërthim** [ʃpərθím]
fight	**përleshje** [pərléʃjɛ]

Call the police!	**Thërrisni policinë!** [θərísni politsínə!]
Please hurry up!	**Ju lutem nxitoni!** [ju lútɛm ndzitóni!]
I'm looking for the police station.	**Kërkoj komisariatin e policisë.** [kərkój komisariátin ɛ politsísə]
I need to make a call.	**Duhet të bëj një telefonatë.** [dúhɛt tə bəj ɲə tɛlɛfonátə]
May I use your phone?	**Mund të përdor telefonin tuaj?** [mund tə pərdór tɛlɛfónin túaj?]

I've been …	**Më …** [mə …]
mugged	**sulmuan** [sulmúan]
robbed	**grabitën** [grabítən]
raped	**përdhunuan** [pərðunúan]
attacked (beaten up)	**rrahën** [ráhən]

Are you all right?	**Jeni mirë?** [jéni mírə?]
Did you see who it was?	**E patë kush ishte?** [ɛ pátə kuʃ íʃtɛ?]
Would you be able to recognize the person?	**Mund ta identifikoni personin?** [mund ta idɛntifikóni pɛrsónin?]
Are you sure?	**Jeni i /e/ sigurt?** [jéni i /ɛ/ sigurt?]

Please calm down.	**Ju lutem qetësohuni.** [ju lútɛm cɛtəsóhuni]
Take it easy!	**Merreni me qetësi!** [mérɛni mɛ cɛtəsí!]
Don't worry!	**Mos u shqetësoni!** [mos u ʃcɛtəsóni!]
Everything will be fine.	**Çdo gjë do rregullohet.** [tʃdo jə do rɛguɫóhɛt]
Everything's all right.	**Çdo gjë është në rregull.** [tʃdo jə əʃtə nə réguɫ]
Come here, please.	**ejani këtu, ju lutem.** [éjani kətú], [ju lútɛm]
I have some questions for you.	**Kam disa pyetje për ju.** [kam disa pýɛtjɛ pər ju]

Wait a moment, please.

Prisni pak, ju lutem.
[prísni pak], [ju lútɛm]

Do you have any I.D.?

A keni ndonjë dokument identifikimi?
[a kéni ndóɲə dokumént idɛntifikími?]

Thanks. You can leave now.

Faleminderit. Mund të largoheni.
[falɛmindérit. mund tə largóhɛni.]

Hands behind your head!

Duart prapa kokës!
[dúart prápa kókəs!]

You're under arrest!

Jeni i /e/ arrestuar!
[jéni i /ɛ/ arɛstúar!]

Health problems

Please help me.	**Ju lutem më ndihmoni.**
	[ju lútɛm mə ndihmóni]
I don't feel well.	**Nuk ndihem mirë.**
	[nuk ndíhɛm mírə]
My husband doesn't feel well.	**Burri im nuk ndjehet mirë.**
	[búri im nuk ndjéhɛt mírə]
My son ...	**Djali im ...**
	[djáli im ...]
My father ...	**Babai im ...**
	[babái im ...]

My wife doesn't feel well.	**Gruaja ime nuk ndihet mirë.**
	[grúaja ímɛ nuk ndíhɛt mírə]
My daughter ...	**Vajza ime ...**
	[vájza ímɛ ...]
My mother ...	**Nëna ime ...**
	[nə́na ímɛ ...]

I've got a ...	**Kam ...**
	[kam ...]
headache	**dhimbje koke**
	[ðímbjɛ kókɛ]
sore throat	**dhimbje fyti**
	[ðímbjɛ fýti]
stomach ache	**dhimbje stomaku**
	[ðímbjɛ stomáku]
toothache	**dhimbje dhëmbi**
	[ðímbjɛ ðə́mbi]

I feel dizzy.	**Ndjehem i /e/ trullosur.**
	[ndjéhɛm i /ɛ/ truɫósur]
He has a fever.	**Ka ethe.**
	[ka éθɛ]
She has a fever.	**Ajo ka ethe.**
	[ajó ka éθɛ]
I can't breathe.	**Nuk marr dot frymë.**
	[nuk mar dot frýmə]

I'm short of breath.	**Mbeta pa frymë.**
	[mbéta pa frýmə]
I am asthmatic.	**unë jam astmatik.**
	[únə jam astmatík]
I am diabetic.	**Jam me diabet.**
	[jam mɛ diabét]

I can't sleep.	**Nuk fle dot.** [nuk flɛ dot]
food poisoning	**helmim nga ushqimi** [hɛlmím ŋa uʃcími]

It hurts here.	**Më dhemb këtu.** [mə ðɛmb kətú]
Help me!	**Ndihmë!** [ndíhmə!]
I am here!	**Jam këtu!** [jam kətú!]
We are here!	**Jemi këtu!** [jémi kətú!]
Get me out of here!	**Më nxirrni nga këtu!** [mə ndzírni ŋa kətú!]
I need a doctor.	**Kam nevojë për doktor.** [kam nɛvójə pər doktór]
I can't move.	**Nuk lëviz dot.** [nuk ləvíz dot]
I can't move my legs.	**Nuk lëviz dot këmbët.** [nuk ləvíz dot kémbət]

I have a wound.	**Jam plagosur.** [jam plagósur]
Is it serious?	**A është serioze?** [a əʃtə sɛriózɛ?]
My documents are in my pocket.	**Dokumentet e mia janë në xhep.** [dokuméntɛt ɛ mía jánə nə dʒép]
Calm down!	**Qetësohuni!** [cɛtəsóhuni!]
May I use your phone?	**Mund të përdor telefonin tuaj?** [mund tə pərdór tɛlɛfónin túaj?]

Call an ambulance!	**Thërrisni një ambulancë!** [θərísni ɲə ambulántsə!]
It's urgent!	**Është urgjente!** [əʃtə urɲéntɛ!]
It's an emergency!	**Është rast urgjent!** [əʃtə rast urɲént!]
Please hurry up!	**Ju lutem nxitoni!** [ju lútɛm ndzitóni!]
Would you please call a doctor?	**Mund të thërrisni një doktor, ju lutem?** [mund tə θərísni ɲə doktór], [ju lútɛm?]
Where is the hospital?	**Ku është spitali?** [ku əʃtə spitáli?]

How are you feeling?	**Si ndiheni?** [si ndíhɛni?]
Are you all right?	**Jeni mirë?** [jéni mírə?]
What's happened?	**Çfarë ndodhi?** [tʃfárə ndóði?]

I feel better now.

Ndihem më mirë tani.
[ndihɛm mə mirə tani]

It's OK.

Është në rregull.
[ə́ʃtə nə régułł]

It's all right.

Është në rregull.
[ə́ʃtə nə régułł]

At the pharmacy

pharmacy (drugstore)	**farmaci** [farmatsí]
24-hour pharmacy	**farmaci 24 orë** [farmatsí nəzét ε kátər orə]
Where is the closest pharmacy?	**Ku është farmacia më e afërt?** [ku ə́ʃtə farmatsía mə ε áfərt?]

Is it open now?	**Është e hapur tani?** [ə́ʃtə ε hápur taní?]
At what time does it open?	**Në çfarë ore hapet?** [nə t͡ʃfárə órε hápɛt?]
At what time does it close?	**Në çfarë ore mbyllet?** [nə t͡ʃfárə órε mbýɫɛt?]

Is it far?	**Është larg?** [ə́ʃtə larg?]
Can I get there on foot?	**Mund të shkoj me këmbë deri atje?** [mund tə ʃkoj mε kə́mbə déri atjé?]
Can you show me on the map?	**Mund të më tregoni në hartë?** [mund tə mə trεgóni nə hártə?]

Please give me something for …	**Ju lutem më jepni diçka për …** [ju lútεm mə jépni ditʃká pər …]
a headache	**dhimbje koke** [ðímbjε kókε]
a cough	**kollë** [kóɫə]
a cold	**ftohje** [ftóhjε]
the flu	**grip** [grip]

a fever	**ethe** [éθε]
a stomach ache	**dhimbje stomaku** [ðímbjε stomáku]
nausea	**të përziera** [tə pərzíεra]
diarrhea	**diarre** [diaré]
constipation	**kapsllëk** [kapsɫ́ək]
pain in the back	**dhimbje në shpinë** [ðímbjε nə ʃpínə]

chest pain	**dhimbje në kraharor** [ðímbjɛ nə kraharór]
side stitch	**dhimbje në brinjë** [ðímbjɛ nə bríɲə]
abdominal pain	**dhimbje barku** [ðímbjɛ bárku]

pill	**pilulë** [pilúlə]
ointment, cream	**vaj, krem** [vaj], [krɛm]
syrup	**shurup** [ʃurúp]
spray	**sprej** [sprɛj]
drops	**pika** [píka]

You need to go to the hospital.	**Duhet të shkoni në spital.** [dúhɛt tə ʃkóni nə spitál]
health insurance	**sigurim shëndetësor** [sigurím ʃəndɛtəsór]
prescription	**recetë** [rɛtsétə]
insect repellant	**mbrojtës nga insektet** [mbrójtəs ŋa inséktɛt]
Band Aid	**leukoplast** [lɛukoplást]

The bare minimum

Excuse me, ...

Më falni, ...
[mə fálni, ...]

Hello.

Përshëndetje.
[pərʃəndétjɛ]

Thank you.

Faleminderit.
[falɛmindérit]

Good bye.

Mirupafshim.
[mirupáfʃim]

Yes.

Po.
[po]

No.

Jo.
[jo]

I don't know.

Nuk e di.
[nuk ɛ di]

Where? | Where to? | When?

Ku? | Për ku? | Kur?
[ku? | pər ku? | kur?]

I need ...

Më nevojitet ...
[mə nɛvojítɛt ...]

I want ...

Dua ...
[dúa ...]

Do you have ...?

Keni ...?
[kéni ...?]

Is there a ... here?

A ka ... këtu?
[a ka ... kətú?]

May I ...?

Mund të ...?
[mund tə ...?]

..., please (polite request)

..., ju lutem
[...], [ju lútɛm]

I'm looking for ...

Kërkoj ...
[kərkój ...]

the restroom

tualet
[tualét]

an ATM

bankomat
[bankomát]

a pharmacy (drugstore)

farmaci
[farmatsí]

a hospital

spital
[spitál]

the police station

komisariat policie
[komisariát politsíɛ]

the subway

metro
[mɛtró]

a taxi	**taksi** [táksi]
the train station	**stacion treni** [statsión trɛni]

My name is ...	**Më quajnë ...** [mə cúajnə ...]
What's your name?	**Si quheni?** [si cúhɛni?]
Could you please help me?	**Ju lutem, mund të ndihmoni?** [ju lútɛm], [mund tə ndihmóni?]
I've got a problem.	**Kam një problem.** [kam ɲə problém]
I don't feel well.	**Nuk ndihem mirë.** [nuk ndihɛm mírə]
Call an ambulance!	**Thërrisni një ambulancë!** [θərísni ɲə ambulántsə!]
May I make a call?	**Mund të bëj një telefonatë?** [mund tə bəj ɲə tɛlɛfonátə?]

I'm sorry.	**Më vjen keq.** [mə vjɛn kɛc]
You're welcome.	**Ju lutem.** [ju lútɛm]

I, me	**unë, mua** [únə], [múa]
you (inform.)	**ti** [ti]
he	**ai** [ai]
she	**ajo** [ajó]
they (masc.)	**ata** [atá]
they (fem.)	**ato** [ató]
we	**ne** [nɛ]
you (pl)	**ju** [ju]
you (sg, form.)	**ju** [ju]

ENTRANCE	**HYRJE** [hýrjɛ]
EXIT	**DALJE** [dáljɛ]
OUT OF ORDER	**NUK FUNKSIONON** [nuk funksionón]
CLOSED	**MBYLLUR** [mbýɫur]

OPEN

HAPUR
[hápur]

FOR WOMEN

PËR FEMRA
[pər fémra]

FOR MEN

PËR MESHKUJ
[pər méʃkuj]

CONCISE
DICTIONARY

This section contains more
than 1,500 useful words
arranged alphabetically.
The dictionary includes a lot
of gastronomic terms and
will be helpful when ordering
food at a restaurant or buying
groceries

T&P Books Publishing

DICTIONARY CONTENTS

T&P Books Publishing

T&P Books Publishing

time	**kohë** (f)	[kóhə]
hour	**orë** (f)	[órə]
half an hour	**gjysmë ore** (f)	[ɟýsmə órɛ]
minute	**minutë** (f)	[minútə]
second	**sekondë** (f)	[sɛkóndə]

today (adv)	**sot**	[sot]
tomorrow (adv)	**nesër**	[nésər]
yesterday (adv)	**dje**	[djé]

Monday	**E hënë** (f)	[ɛ hénə]
Tuesday	**E martë** (f)	[ɛ mártə]
Wednesday	**E mërkurë** (f)	[ɛ mərkúrə]
Thursday	**E enjte** (f)	[ɛ éɲtɛ]
Friday	**E premte** (f)	[ɛ prémtɛ]
Saturday	**E shtunë** (f)	[ɛ ʃtúnə]
Sunday	**E dielë** (f)	[ɛ díɛlə]

day	**ditë** (f)	[dítə]
working day	**ditë pune** (f)	[dítə púnɛ]
public holiday	**festë kombëtare** (f)	[féstə kombətárɛ]
weekend	**fundjavë** (f)	[fundjávə]

week	**javë** (f)	[jávə]
last week (adv)	**javën e kaluar**	[jávən ɛ kalúar]
next week (adv)	**javën e ardhshme**	[jávən ɛ árðʃmɛ]

sunrise	**agim** (m)	[agím]
sunset	**perëndim dielli** (m)	[pɛrəndím diéɫi]

in the morning	**në mëngjes**	[nə məɲɟés]
in the afternoon	**pasdite**	[pasdítɛ]

in the evening	**në mbrëmje**	[nə mbrémjɛ]
tonight (this evening)	**sonte në mbrëmje**	[sóntɛ nə mbrəmjɛ]

at night	**natën**	[nátən]
midnight	**mesnatë** (f)	[mɛsnátə]

January	**Janar** (m)	[janár]
February	**Shkurt** (m)	[ʃkurt]
March	**Mars** (m)	[mars]
April	**Prill** (m)	[priɫ]
May	**Maj** (m)	[maj]
June	**Qershor** (m)	[cɛrʃór]

July	Korrik (m)	[korík]
August	Gusht (m)	[guʃt]
September	Shtator (m)	[ʃtatór]
October	Tetor (m)	[tɛtór]
November	Nëntor (m)	[nəntór]
December	Dhjetor (m)	[ðjɛtór]

in spring	në pranverë	[nə pranvérə]
in summer	në verë	[nə vérə]
in fall	në vjeshtë	[nə vjéʃtə]
in winter	në dimër	[nə dímər]

month	muaj (m)	[múaj]
season (summer, etc.)	stinë (f)	[stínə]
year	vit (m)	[vit]
century	shekull (m)	[ʃékuɫ]

2. Numbers. Numerals

digit, figure	shifër (f)	[ʃífər]
number	numër (m)	[númər]
minus sign	minus (m)	[minús]
plus sign	plus (m)	[plus]
sum, total	shuma (f)	[ʃúma]

first (adj)	i pari	[i pári]
second (adj)	i dyti	[i dýti]
third (adj)	i treti	[i tréti]

0 zero	zero	[zéro]
1 one	një	[ɲə]
2 two	dy	[dy]
3 three	tre	[trɛ]
4 four	katër	[kátər]

5 five	pesë	[pésə]
6 six	gjashtë	[ɟáʃtə]
7 seven	shtatë	[ʃtátə]
8 eight	tetë	[tétə]
9 nine	nëntë	[nəntə]
10 ten	dhjetë	[ðjétə]

11 eleven	njëmbëdhjetë	[ɲəmbəðjétə]
12 twelve	dymbëdhjetë	[dymbəðjétə]
13 thirteen	trembëdhjetë	[trɛmbəðjétə]
14 fourteen	katërmbëdhjetë	[katərmbəðjétə]
15 fifteen	pesëmbëdhjetë	[pɛsəmbəðjétə]

| 16 sixteen | gjashtëmbëdhjetë | [ɟaʃtəmbəðjétə] |
| 17 seventeen | shtatëmbëdhjetë | [ʃtatəmbəðjétə] |

18 eighteen	tetëmbëdhjetë	[tɛtəmbəðjétə]
19 nineteen	nëntëmbëdhjetë	[nəntəmbəðjétə]

20 twenty	njëzet	[ɲəzét]
30 thirty	tridhjetë	[triðjétə]
40 forty	dyzet	[dyzét]
50 fifty	pesëdhjetë	[pɛsəðjétə]

60 sixty	gjashtëdhjetë	[ɟaʃtəðjétə]
70 seventy	shtatëdhjetë	[ʃtatəðjétə]
80 eighty	tetëdhjetë	[tɛtəðjétə]
90 ninety	nëntëdhjetë	[nəntəðjétə]

100 one hundred	njëqind	[ɲəcínd]
200 two hundred	dyqind	[dycínd]
300 three hundred	treqind	[trɛcínd]
400 four hundred	katërqind	[katərcínd]
500 five hundred	pesëqind	[pɛsəcínd]

600 six hundred	gjashtëqind	[ɟaʃtəcínd]
700 seven hundred	shtatëqind	[ʃtatəcínd]
800 eight hundred	tetëqind	[tɛtəcínd]
900 nine hundred	nëntëqind	[nəntəcínd]
1000 one thousand	një mijë	[ɲə míjə]

10000 ten thousand	dhjetë mijë	[ðjétə míjə]
one hundred thousand	njëqind mijë	[ɲəcínd míjə]

million	milion (m)	[milión]
billion	miliardë (f)	[miliárdə]

3. Humans. Family

man (adult male)	burrë (m)	[búrə]
young man	djalë i ri (m)	[djálə i rí]
teenager	adoleshent (m)	[adolɛʃént]
woman	grua (f)	[grúa]
girl (young woman)	vajzë (f)	[vájzə]

age	moshë (f)	[móʃə]
adult (adj)	i rritur	[i rítur]
middle-aged (adj)	mesoburrë	[mɛsobúrə]
elderly (adj)	i moshuar	[i moʃúar]
old (adj)	i vjetër	[i vjétər]

old man	plak (m)	[plak]
old woman	plakë (f)	[plákə]
retirement	pension (m)	[pɛnsión]
to retire (from job)	dal në pension	[dál nə pɛnsión]
retiree	pensionist (m)	[pɛnsioníst]

mother	nënë (f)	[nə́nə]
father	baba (f)	[babá]
son	bir (m)	[bir]
daughter	bijë (f)	[bíjə]
brother	vëlla (m)	[vəɫá]
elder brother	vëllai i madh (m)	[vəɫái i mað]
younger brother	vëllai i vogël (m)	[vəɫai i vógəl]
sister	motër (f)	[mótər]
elder sister	motra e madhe (f)	[mótra ɛ máðɛ]
younger sister	motra e vogël (f)	[mótra ɛ vógəl]

parents	prindër (pl)	[príndər]
child	fëmijë (f)	[fəmíjə]
children	fëmijë (pl)	[fəmíjə]
stepmother	njerkë (f)	[ɲérkə]
stepfather	njerk (m)	[ɲérk]

grandmother	gjyshe (f)	[ɟýʃɛ]
grandfather	gjysh (m)	[ɟyʃ]
grandson	nip (m)	[nip]
granddaughter	mbesë (f)	[mbésə]
grandchildren	nipër e mbesa (pl)	[nípər ɛ mbésa]
uncle	dajë (f)	[dájə]
aunt	teze (f)	[tézɛ]
nephew	nip (m)	[nip]
niece	mbesë (f)	[mbésə]

wife	bashkëshorte (f)	[baʃkəʃórtɛ]
husband	bashkëshort (m)	[baʃkəʃórt]
married (masc.)	i martuar	[i martúar]
married (fem.)	e martuar	[ɛ martúar]
widow	vejushë (f)	[vɛjúʃə]
widower	vejan (m)	[vɛján]

| name (first name) | emër (m) | [émər] |
| surname (last name) | mbiemër (m) | [mbiémər] |

relative	kushëri (m)	[kuʃərí]
friend (masc.)	mik (m)	[mik]
friendship	miqësi (f)	[micəsí]

partner	partner (m)	[partnér]
superior (n)	epror (m)	[ɛprór]
colleague	koleg (m)	[kolég]
neighbors	komshinj (pl)	[komʃíɲ]

4. Human body

| organism (body) | organizëm (m) | [organízəm] |
| body | trup (m) | [trup] |

heart	zemër (f)	[zémər]
blood	gjak (m)	[ɟak]
brain	tru (m)	[tru]
nerve	nerv (m)	[nɛrv]

bone	kockë (f)	[kótskə]
skeleton	skelet (m)	[skɛlét]
spine (backbone)	shtyllë kurrizore (f)	[ʃtýɫə kurizórɛ]
rib	brinjë (f)	[bríɲə]
skull	kafkë (f)	[káfkə]

muscle	muskul (m)	[múskul]
lungs	mushkëri (m)	[muʃkərí]
skin	lëkurë (f)	[ləkúrə]

head	kokë (f)	[kókə]
face	fytyrë (f)	[fytýrə]
nose	hundë (f)	[húndə]
forehead	ball (m)	[báɫ]
cheek	faqe (f)	[fácɛ]

mouth	gojë (f)	[gójə]
tongue	gjuhë (f)	[ɟúhə]
tooth	dhëmb (m)	[ðəmb]
lips	buzë (f)	[búzə]
chin	mjekër (f)	[mjékər]

ear	vesh (m)	[vɛʃ]
neck	qafë (f)	[cáfə]
throat	fyt (m)	[fyt]

eye	sy (m)	[sy]
pupil	bebëz (f)	[bébəz]
eyebrow	vetull (f)	[vétuɫ]
eyelash	qerpik (m)	[cɛrpík]

hair	flokë (pl)	[flókə]
hairstyle	model flokësh (m)	[modél flókəʃ]
mustache	mustaqe (f)	[mustácɛ]
beard	mjekër (f)	[mjékər]
to have (a beard, etc.)	lë mjekër	[lə mjékər]
bald (adj)	qeros	[cɛrós]

hand	dorë (f)	[dórə]
arm	krah (m)	[krah]
finger	gisht i dorës (m)	[gíʃt i dórəs]
nail	thua (f)	[θúa]
palm	pëllëmbë dore (f)	[pəɫəmbə dórɛ]

shoulder	shpatull (f)	[ʃpátuɫ]
leg	këmbë (f)	[kémbə]
foot	shputë (f)	[ʃpútə]

| knee | gju (m) | [ɲú] |
| heel | thembër (f) | [θémbər] |

back	kurriz (m)	[kuríz]
waist	beli (m)	[béli]
beauty mark	nishan (m)	[niʃán]
birthmark	shenjë lindjeje (f)	[ʃéɲə líndjɛjɛ]
(café au lait spot)		

5. Medicine. Diseases. Drugs

health	shëndet (m)	[ʃəndét]
well (not sick)	mirë	[mírə]
sickness	sëmundje (f)	[səmúndjɛ]
to be sick	jam sëmurë	[jam səmúrə]
ill, sick (adj)	i sëmurë	[i səmúrə]

cold (illness)	ftohje (f)	[ftóhjɛ]
to catch a cold	ftohem	[ftóhɛm]
tonsillitis	grykët (m)	[grýkət]
pneumonia	pneumoni (f)	[pnɛumoní]
flu, influenza	grip (m)	[grip]

runny nose (coryza)	rrifë (f)	[rífə]
cough	kollë (f)	[kóɫə]
to cough (vi)	kollitem	[koɫítɛm]
to sneeze (vi)	teshtij	[tɛʃtíj]

stroke	goditje (f)	[godítjɛ]
heart attack	sulm në zemër (m)	[sulm nə zémər]
allergy	alergji (f)	[alɛrɟí]
asthma	astmë (f)	[ástmə]
diabetes	diabet (m)	[diabét]

tumor	tumor (m)	[tumór]
cancer	kancer (m)	[kantsér]
alcoholism	alkoolizëm (m)	[alkoolízəm]
AIDS	SIDA (f)	[sída]
fever	ethe (f)	[éθɛ]
seasickness	sëmundje deti (f)	[səmúndjɛ déti]

bruise (hématome)	mavijosje (f)	[mavijósjɛ]
bump (lump)	gungë (f)	[gúŋə]
to limp (vi)	çaloj	[tʃalój]
dislocation	dislokim (m)	[dislokím]
to dislocate (vt)	del nga vendi	[dɛl ŋa véndi]

fracture	thyerje (f)	[θýɛrjɛ]
burn (injury)	djegie (f)	[djégiɛ]
injury	dëmtim (m)	[dəmtím]

| pain, ache | dhimbje (f) | [ðímbjɛ] |
| toothache | dhimbje dhëmbi (f) | [ðímbjɛ ðə́mbi] |

to sweat (perspire)	djersij	[djɛrsíj]
deaf (adj)	shurdh	[ʃurð]
mute (adj)	memec	[mɛméts]

immunity	imunitet (m)	[imunitét]
virus	virus (m)	[virús]
microbe	mikrob (m)	[mikrób]
bacterium	bakterie (f)	[baktériɛ]
infection	infeksion (m)	[infɛksión]

hospital	spital (m)	[spitál]
cure	kurë (f)	[kúrə]
to vaccinate (vt)	vaksinoj	[vaksinój]
to be in a coma	jam në komë	[jam nə kómə]
intensive care	kujdes intensiv (m)	[kujdés intɛnsív]
symptom	simptomë (f)	[simptómə]
pulse (heartbeat)	puls (m)	[puls]

6. Feelings. Emotions. Conversation

I, me	Unë, mua	[unə], [múa]
you	ti, ty	[ti], [ty]
he	ai	[aí]
she	ajo	[ajó]
it	ai	[aí]

we	ne	[nɛ]
you (to a group)	ju	[ju]
they (masc.)	ata	[atá]
they (fem.)	ato	[ató]

Hello! (fam.)	Përshëndetje!	[pərʃəndétjɛ!]
Hello! (form.)	Përshëndetje!	[pərʃəndétjɛ!]
Good morning!	Mirëmëngjes!	[mirəmənɟés!]
Good afternoon!	Mirëdita!	[mirədíta!]
Good evening!	Mirëmbrëma!	[mirəmbréma!]

to say hello	përshëndes	[pərʃəndés]
to greet (vt)	përshëndes	[pərʃəndés]
How are you? (form.)	Si jeni?	[si jéni?]
How are you? (fam.)	Si je?	[si jɛ?]
Goodbye!	Mirupafshim!	[mirupáfʃim!]
Bye!	U pafshim!	[u páfʃim!]
Thank you!	Faleminderit!	[falɛmindérit!]

| feelings | ndjenja (pl) | [ndjéɲa] |
| to be hungry | kam uri | [kam urí] |

| to be thirsty | kam etje | [kam étjɛ] |
| tired (adj) | i lodhur | [i lóður] |

to be worried	shqetësohem	[ʃcɛtəsóhɛm]
to be nervous	nervozohem	[nɛrvozóhɛm]
hope	shpresë (f)	[ʃprésə]
to hope (vi, vt)	shpresoj	[ʃprɛsój]

character	karakter (m)	[karaktér]
modest (adj)	modest	[modést]
lazy (adj)	dembel	[dɛmbél]
generous (adj)	zemërgjerë	[zɛmərɟérə]
talented (adj)	i talentuar	[i talɛntúar]

honest (adj)	i ndershëm	[i ndérʃəm]
serious (adj)	serioz	[sɛrióz]
shy, timid (adj)	i turpshëm	[i túrpʃəm]
sincere (adj)	i sinqertë	[i sincértə]
coward	frikacak (m)	[frikatsák]

to sleep (vi)	fle	[flɛ]
dream	ëndërr (m)	[əndər]
bed	shtrat (m)	[ʃtrat]
pillow	jastëk (m)	[jasték]

insomnia	pagjumësi (f)	[paɟuməsí]
to go to bed	shkoj të fle	[ʃkoj tə flɛ]
nightmare	ankth (m)	[ankθ]
alarm clock	orë me zile (f)	[órə mɛ zílɛ]

smile	buzëqeshje (f)	[buzəcéʃʃɛ]
to smile (vi)	buzëqesh	[buzəcéʃ]
to laugh (vi)	qesh	[cɛʃ]

quarrel	grindje (f)	[gríndjɛ]
insult	ofendim (m)	[ofɛndím]
resentment	fyerje (f)	[fýɛrjɛ]
angry (mad)	i zemëruar	[i zɛmərúar]

7. Clothing. Personal accessories

clothes	rroba (f)	[róba]
coat (overcoat)	pallto (f)	[páɫto]
fur coat	gëzof (m)	[gəzóf]
jacket (e.g., leather ~)	xhaketë (f)	[dʒakétə]
raincoat (trenchcoat, etc.)	pardesy (f)	[pardɛsý]

shirt (button shirt)	këmishë (f)	[kəmíʃə]
pants	pantallona (f)	[pantaɫóna]
suit jacket	xhaketë kostumi (f)	[dʒakétə kostúmi]

suit	kostum (m)	[kostúm]
dress (frock)	fustan (m)	[fustán]
skirt	fund (m)	[fund]
T-shirt	bluzë (f)	[blúzə]
bathrobe	peshqir trupi (m)	[pɛʃcír trúpi]
pajamas	pizhame (f)	[piʒámɛ]
workwear	rroba pune (f)	[róba púnɛ]

underwear	të brendshme (f)	[tə bréndʃmɛ]
socks	çorape (pl)	[tʃorápɛ]
bra	sytjena (f)	[sytjéna]
pantyhose	geta (f)	[géta]
stockings (thigh highs)	çorape të holla (pl)	[tʃorápɛ tə hóła]
bathing suit	rrobë banje (f)	[róbə báɲɛ]

hat	kapelë (f)	[kapélə]
footwear	këpucë (pl)	[kəpútsə]
boots (e.g., cowboy ~)	çizme (pl)	[tʃízmɛ]
heel	takë (f)	[tákə]
shoestring	lidhëse këpucësh (f)	[líðəsɛ kəpútsəʃ]
shoe polish	bojë këpucësh (f)	[bójə kəpútsəʃ]

cotton (n)	pambuk (m)	[pambúk]
wool (n)	lesh (m)	[lɛʃ]
fur (n)	gëzof (m)	[gəzóf]

gloves	dorëza (pl)	[dórəza]
mittens	doreza (f)	[doréza]
scarf (muffler)	shall (m)	[ʃał]
glasses (eyeglasses)	syze (f)	[sýzɛ]
umbrella	çadër (f)	[tʃádər]

| tie (necktie) | kravatë (f) | [kravátə] |
| handkerchief | shami (f) | [ʃamí] |

| comb | krehër (m) | [kréhər] |
| hairbrush | furçë flokësh (f) | [fúrtʃə flókəʃ] |

buckle	tokëz (f)	[tókəz]
belt	rrip (m)	[rip]
purse	çantë (f)	[tʃántə]

| collar | jakë (f) | [jákə] |
| pocket | xhep (m) | [dʒɛp] |

| sleeve | mëngë (f) | [méŋə] |
| fly (on trousers) | zinxhir (m) | [zindʒír] |

zipper (fastener)	zinxhir (m)	[zindʒír]
button	kopsë (f)	[kópsə]
to get dirty (vi)	bëhem pis	[béhɛm pis]
stain (mark, spot)	njollë (f)	[ɲółə]

8. City. Urban institutions

store	dyqan (m)	[dycán]
shopping mall	qendër tregtare (f)	[céndər trɛgtárɛ]
supermarket	supermarket (m)	[supɛrmarkét]
shoe store	dyqan këpucësh (m)	[dycán kəpútsəʃ]
bookstore	librari (f)	[librarí]

drugstore, pharmacy	farmaci (f)	[farmatsí]
bakery	furrë (f)	[fúrə]
pastry shop	pastiçeri (f)	[pastitʃɛrí]
grocery store	dyqan ushqimor (m)	[dycán uʃcimór]
butcher shop	dyqan mishi (m)	[dycán míʃi]
produce store	dyqan fruta-perimesh (m)	[dycán frúta-pɛrímɛʃ]
market	treg (m)	[trɛg]

hair salon	parukeri (f)	[parukɛrí]
post office	zyrë postare (f)	[zýrə postárɛ]
dry cleaners	pastrim kimik (m)	[pastrím kimík]
circus	cirk (m)	[tsírk]
zoo	kopsht zoologjik (m)	[kópʃt zooloɟík]

theater	teatër (m)	[tɛátər]
movie theater	kinema (f)	[kinɛmá]
museum	muze (m)	[muzé]
library	bibliotekë (f)	[bibliotékə]

mosque	xhami (f)	[dʒamí]
synagogue	sinagogë (f)	[sinagógə]
cathedral	katedrale (f)	[katɛdrálɛ]
temple	tempull (m)	[témpuł]
church	kishë (f)	[kíʃə]

college	kolegj (m)	[koléɟ]
university	universitet (m)	[univɛrsitét]
school	shkollë (f)	[ʃkółə]

hotel	hotel (m)	[hotél]
bank	bankë (f)	[bánkə]
embassy	ambasadë (f)	[ambasádə]
travel agency	agjenci udhëtimesh (f)	[aɟɛntsí uðətímɛʃ]

subway	metro (f)	[mɛtró]
hospital	spital (m)	[spitál]
gas station	pikë karburanti (f)	[píkə karburánti]
parking lot	parking (m)	[parkíŋ]

ENTRANCE	HYRJE	[hýrjɛ]
EXIT	DALJE	[dáljɛ]
PUSH	SHTY	[ʃty]
PULL	TËRHIQ	[tərhíc]

83

OPEN	HAPUR	[hápur]
CLOSED	MBYLLUR	[mbýɫur]

monument	monument (m)	[monumént]
fortress	kala (f)	[kalá]
palace	pallat (m)	[paɫát]

medieval (adj)	mesjetare	[mɛsjɛtárɛ]
ancient (adj)	e lashtë	[ɛ láʃtə]
national (adj)	kombëtare	[kombətárɛ]
famous (monument, etc.)	i famshëm	[i fámʃəm]

9. Money. Finances

money	para (f)	[pará]
coin	monedhë (f)	[monéðə]
dollar	dollar (m)	[doɫár]
euro	euro (f)	[éuro]

ATM	bankomat (m)	[bankomát]
currency exchange	këmbim valutor (m)	[kəmbím valutór]
exchange rate	kurs këmbimi (m)	[kurs kəmbími]
cash	kesh (m)	[kɛʃ]

How much?	Sa?	[sa?]
to pay (vi, vt)	paguaj	[pagúaj]
payment	pagesë (f)	[pagésə]
change (give the ~)	kusur (m)	[kusúr]

price	çmim (m)	[tʃmím]
discount	ulje (f)	[úljɛ]
cheap (adj)	e lirë	[ɛ lírə]
expensive (adj)	i shtrenjtë	[i ʃtréɲtə]

bank	bankë (f)	[bánkə]
account	llogari (f)	[ɫogarí]
credit card	kartë krediti (f)	[kártə krɛdíti]
check	çek (m)	[tʃɛk]
to write a check	lëshoj një çek	[ləʃój ɲə tʃék]
checkbook	bllok çeqesh (m)	[bɫók tʃécɛʃ]

debt	borxh (m)	[bórdʒ]
debtor	debitor (m)	[dɛbitór]
to lend (money)	jap hua	[jap huá]
to borrow (vi, vt)	marr hua	[mar huá]

to rent (~ a tuxedo)	marr me qira	[mar mɛ cirá]
on credit (adv)	me kredi	[mɛ krɛdí]
wallet	portofol (m)	[portofól]
safe	kasafortë (f)	[kasafórtə]

| inheritance | trashëgimi (f) | [traʃəgimí] |
| fortune (wealth) | pasuri (f) | [pasurí] |

tax	taksë (f)	[táksə]
fine	gjobë (f)	[ɟóbə]
to fine (vt)	vendos gjobë	[vɛndós ɟóbə]

wholesale (adj)	me shumicë	[mɛ ʃumítsə]
retail (adj)	me pakicë	[mɛ pakítsə]
to insure (vt)	siguroj	[sigurój]
insurance	sigurim (m)	[sigurím]

capital	kapital (m)	[kapitál]
turnover	qarkullim (m)	[carkuɬím]
stock (share)	stok (m)	[stok]
profit	fitim (m)	[fitím]
profitable (adj)	fitimprurës	[fitimprúrəs]

crisis	krizë (f)	[krízə]
bankruptcy	falimentim (m)	[falimɛntím]
to go bankrupt	falimentoj	[falimɛntój]

accountant	kontabilist (m)	[kontabilíst]
salary	pagë (f)	[págə]
bonus (money)	bonus (m)	[bonús]

10. Transportation

bus	autobus (m)	[autobús]
streetcar	tramvaj (m)	[tramváj]
trolley bus	autobus tramvaj (m)	[autobús tramváj]

to go by ...	udhëtoj me ...	[uðətój mɛ ...]
to get on (~ the bus)	hip	[hip]
to get off ...	zbres ...	[zbrɛs ...]

stop (e.g., bus ~)	stacion (m)	[statsión]
terminus	terminal (m)	[tɛrminál]
schedule	orar (m)	[orár]
ticket	biletë (f)	[bilétə]
to be late (for ...)	vonohem	[vonóhɛm]

taxi, cab	taksi (m)	[táksi]
by taxi	me taksi	[mɛ táksi]
taxi stand	stacion taksish (m)	[statsión táksiʃ]

traffic	trafik (m)	[trafík]
rush hour	orë e trafikut të rëndë (f)	[órə ɛ trafíkut tə rəndə]
to park (vi)	parkoj	[parkój]
subway	metro (f)	[mɛtró]

85

station	stacion (m)	[statsión]
train	tren (m)	[trɛn]
train station	stacion treni (m)	[statsión tréni]
rails	shina (pl)	[ʃína]
compartment	ndarje (f)	[ndárjɛ]
berth	kat (m)	[kat]

airplane	avion (m)	[avión]
air ticket	biletë avioni (f)	[bilétə avióni]
airline	kompani ajrore (f)	[kompaní ajrórɛ]
airport	aeroport (m)	[aɛropórt]

flight (act of flying)	fluturim (m)	[fluturím]
luggage	bagazh (m)	[bagáʒ]
luggage cart	karrocë bagazhesh (f)	[karótsə bagáʒɛʃ]

ship	anije (f)	[aníjɛ]
cruise ship	krocierë (f)	[krotsiérə]
yacht	jaht (m)	[jáht]
boat (flat-bottomed ~)	barkë (f)	[bárkə]

captain	kapiten (m)	[kapitén]
cabin	kabinë (f)	[kabínə]
port (harbor)	port (m)	[port]

bicycle	biçikletë (f)	[bitʃiklétə]
scooter	skuter (m)	[skutér]
motorcycle, bike	motoçikletë (f)	[mototʃiklétə]
pedal	pedale (f)	[pɛdálɛ]
pump	pompë (f)	[pómpə]
wheel	rrotë (f)	[rótə]

automobile, car	makinë (f)	[makínə]
ambulance	ambulancë (f)	[ambulántsə]
truck	kamion (m)	[kamión]
used (adj)	i përdorur	[i pərdórur]
car crash	aksident (m)	[aksidént]
repair	riparim (m)	[riparím]

11. Food. Part 1

meat	mish (m)	[miʃ]
chicken	pulë (f)	[púlə]
duck	rosë (f)	[rósə]

pork	mish derri (m)	[miʃ déri]
veal	mish viçi (m)	[miʃ vítʃi]
lamb	mish qengji (m)	[miʃ cénɟi]
beef	mish lope (m)	[miʃ lópɛ]
sausage (bologna, etc.)	salsiçe (f)	[salsítʃɛ]

egg	ve (f)	[vɛ]
fish	peshk (m)	[pɛʃk]
cheese	djath (m)	[djáθ]
sugar	sheqer (m)	[ʃɛcér]
salt	kripë (f)	[krípə]

rice	oriz (m)	[oríz]
pasta (macaroni)	makarona (f)	[makaróna]
butter	gjalp (m)	[ɟalp]
vegetable oil	vaj vegjetal (m)	[vaj vɛɟɛtál]
bread	bukë (f)	[búkə]
chocolate (n)	çokollatë (f)	[tʃokołátə]

wine	verë (f)	[vérə]
coffee	kafe (f)	[káfɛ]
milk	qumësht (m)	[cúməʃt]
juice	lëng frutash (m)	[ləŋ frútaʃ]

| beer | birrë (f) | [bírə] |
| tea | çaj (m) | [tʃáj] |

tomato	domate (f)	[domátɛ]
cucumber	kastravec (m)	[kastravéts]
carrot	karotë (f)	[karótə]
potato	patate (f)	[patátɛ]

| onion | qepë (f) | [cépə] |
| garlic | hudhër (f) | [húðər] |

cabbage	lakër (f)	[lákər]
beet	panxhar (m)	[pandʒár]
eggplant	patëllxhan (m)	[patəłdʒán]
dill	kopër (f)	[kópər]

| lettuce | sallatë jeshile (f) | [sałátə jɛʃílɛ] |
| corn (maize) | misër (m) | [mísər] |

fruit	frut (m)	[frut]
apple	mollë (f)	[mółə]
pear	dardhë (f)	[dárðə]
lemon	limon (m)	[limón]

| orange | portokall (m) | [portokáł] |
| strawberry (garden ~) | luleshtrydhe (f) | [lulɛʃtrýðɛ] |

plum	kumbull (f)	[kúmbuł]
raspberry	mjedër (f)	[mjédər]
pineapple	ananas (m)	[ananás]
banana	banane (f)	[banánɛ]
watermelon	shalqi (m)	[ʃalcí]
grape	rrush (m)	[ruʃ]
melon	pjepër (m)	[pjépər]

12. Food. Part 2

cuisine	kuzhinë (f)	[kuʒínə]
recipe	recetë (f)	[rɛtsétə]
food	ushqim (m)	[uʃcím]

to have breakfast	ha mëngjes	[ha mənɟés]
to have lunch	ha drekë	[ha drékə]
to have dinner	ha darkë	[ha dárkə]

taste, flavor	shije (f)	[ʃíjɛ]
tasty (adj)	i shijshëm	[i ʃíjʃəm]
cold (adj)	i ftohtë	[i ftóhtə]
hot (adj)	i nxehtë	[i ndzéhtə]
sweet (sugary)	i ëmbël	[i émbəl]
salty (adj)	i kripur	[i krípur]

sandwich (bread)	sandviç (m)	[sandvítʃ]
side dish	garniturë (f)	[garnitúrə]
filling (for cake, pie)	mbushje (f)	[mbúʃjɛ]
sauce	salcë (f)	[sáltsə]
piece (of cake, pie)	copë (f)	[tsópə]

diet	dietë (f)	[diétə]
vitamin	vitaminë (f)	[vitamínə]
calorie	kalori (f)	[kalorí]
vegetarian (n)	vegjetarian (m)	[vɛɟɛtarián]

restaurant	restorant (m)	[rɛstoránt]
coffee house	kafene (f)	[kafɛné]
appetite	oreks (m)	[oréks]
Enjoy your meal!	Të bëftë mirë!	[tə bəftə mírə!]

waiter	kamerier (m)	[kamɛriér]
waitress	kameriere (f)	[kamɛriérɛ]
bartender	banakier (m)	[banakiér]
menu	menu (f)	[mɛnú]

spoon	lugë (f)	[lúgə]
knife	thikë (f)	[θíkə]
fork	pirun (m)	[pirún]
cup (e.g., coffee ~)	filxhan (m)	[fildʒán]

plate (dinner ~)	pjatë (f)	[pjátə]
saucer	pjatë filxhani (f)	[pjátə fildʒáni]
napkin (on table)	pecetë (f)	[pɛtsétə]
toothpick	kruajtëse dhëmbësh (f)	[krúajtəsɛ ðémbəʃ]

to order (meal)	porosis	[porosís]
course, dish	pjatë (f)	[pjátə]
portion	racion (m)	[ratsión]

appetizer	antipastë (f)	[antipástə]
salad	sallatë (f)	[saɫátə]
soup	supë (f)	[súpə]

dessert	ëmbëlsirë (f)	[əmbəlsírə]
jam (whole fruit jam)	reçel (m)	[rɛtʃél]
ice-cream	akullore (f)	[akuɫórɛ]

check	faturë (f)	[fatúrə]
to pay the check	paguaj faturën	[pagúaj fatúrən]
tip	bakshish (m)	[bakʃíʃ]

13. House. Apartment. Part 1

house	shtëpi (f)	[ʃtəpí]
country house	vilë (f)	[vílə]
villa (seaside ~)	vilë (f)	[vílə]

floor, story	kat (m)	[kat]
entrance	hyrje (f)	[hýrjɛ]
wall	mur (m)	[murɾ]
roof	çati (f)	[tʃatí]
chimney	oxhak (m)	[odʒák]

attic (storage place)	papafingo (f)	[papafíŋo]
window	dritare (f)	[dritárɛ]
window ledge	prag dritareje (m)	[prag dritárɛjɛ]
balcony	ballkon (m)	[baɫkón]

stairs (stairway)	shkallë (f)	[ʃkáɫə]
mailbox	kuti postare (f)	[kutí postárɛ]
garbage can	kazan mbeturinash (m)	[kazán mbɛturínaʃ]
elevator	ashensor (m)	[aʃɛnsór]

electricity	elektricitet (m)	[ɛlɛktritsitét]
light bulb	poç (m)	[potʃ]
switch	çelës drite (m)	[tʃéləs drítɛ]
wall socket	prizë (f)	[prízə]
fuse	siguresë (f)	[sigurésə]

door	derë (f)	[dérə]
handle, doorknob	dorezë (f)	[dorézə]
key	çelës (m)	[tʃéləs]
doormat	tapet hyrës (m)	[tapét hýrəs]

door lock	kyç (m)	[kytʃ]
doorbell	zile (f)	[zílɛ]
knock (at the door)	trokitje (f)	[trokítjɛ]
to knock (vi)	trokas	[trokás]
peephole	vrimë përgjimi (f)	[vrímə pərɟími]

yard	oborr (m)	[obór]
garden	kopsht (m)	[kopʃt]
swimming pool	pishinë (f)	[piʃínə]
gym (home gym)	palestër (f)	[paléstər]
tennis court	fushë tenisi (f)	[fúʃə tɛnísi]
garage	garazh (m)	[garáʒ]

private property	pronë private (f)	[prónə privátɛ]
warning sign	shenjë paralajmëruese (f)	[ʃéɲə paralajmərúɛsɛ]
security	sigurim (m)	[sigurím]
security guard	roje sigurimi (m)	[rójɛ sigurími]

renovations	renovim (m)	[rɛnovím]
to renovate (vt)	rinovoj	[rinovój]
to put in order	rregulloj	[rɛguɫój]
to paint (~ a wall)	lyej	[lýɛj]
wallpaper	tapiceri (f)	[tapitsɛrí]
to varnish (vt)	lustroj	[lustrój]

pipe	gyp (m)	[gyp]
tools	vegla (pl)	[végla]
basement	qilar (m)	[cilár]
sewerage (system)	kanalizim (m)	[kanalizím]

14. House. Apartment. Part 2

apartment	apartament (m)	[apartamént]
room	dhomë (f)	[ðómə]
bedroom	dhomë gjumi (f)	[ðómə ɟúmi]
dining room	dhomë ngrënie (f)	[ðómə ŋrəníɛ]

living room	dhomë ndeje (f)	[ðómə ndéjɛ]
study (home office)	dhomë pune (f)	[ðómə púnɛ]
entry room	hyrje (f)	[hýrjɛ]
bathroom (room with a bath or shower)	banjo (f)	[báɲo]
half bath	tualet (m)	[tualét]

floor	dysheme (f)	[dyʃɛmé]
ceiling	tavan (m)	[taván]

to dust (vt)	marr pluhurat	[mar plúhurat]
vacuum cleaner	fshesë elektrike (f)	[fʃésə ɛlɛktríkɛ]
to vacuum (vt)	thith pluhurin	[θiθ plúhurin]

mop	shtupë (f)	[ʃtúpə]
dust cloth	leckë (f)	[létskə]
short broom	fshesë (f)	[fʃésə]
dustpan	kaci (f)	[katsí]
furniture	orendi (f)	[orɛndí]

table	tryezë (f)	[tryézə]
chair	karrige (f)	[karígɛ]
armchair	kolltuk (m)	[koɬtúk]

bookcase	raft librash (m)	[ráft líbraʃ]
shelf	sergjen (m)	[sɛrɟén]
wardrobe	gardërobë (f)	[gardəróbə]

mirror	pasqyrë (f)	[pascýrə]
carpet	qilim (m)	[cilím]
fireplace	oxhak (m)	[odʒák]
drapes	perde (f)	[pérdɛ]
table lamp	llambë tavoline (f)	[ɬámbə tavolínɛ]
chandelier	llambadar (m)	[ɬambadár]

kitchen	kuzhinë (f)	[kuʒínə]
gas stove (range)	sobë me gaz (f)	[sóbə mɛ gaz]
electric stove	sobë elektrike (f)	[sóbə ɛlɛktríkɛ]
microwave oven	mikrovalë (f)	[mikroválə]

refrigerator	frigorifer (m)	[frigorifér]
freezer	frigorifer (m)	[frigorifér]
dishwasher	pjatalarëse (f)	[pjatalárəsɛ]
faucet	rubinet (m)	[rubinét]

meat grinder	grirëse mishi (f)	[grírəsɛ míʃi]
juicer	shtrydhëse frutash (f)	[ʃtrýðəsɛ frútaʃ]
toaster	toster (m)	[tostér]
mixer	mikser (m)	[miksér]

coffee machine	makinë kafeje (f)	[makínə kaféjɛ]
kettle	çajnik (m)	[tʃajník]
teapot	çajnik (m)	[tʃajník]

TV set	televizor (m)	[tɛlɛvizór]
VCR (video recorder)	video regjistrues (m)	[vídɛo rɛɟistrúɛs]
iron (e.g., steam ~)	hekur (m)	[hékur]
telephone	telefon (m)	[tɛlɛfón]

15. Professions. Social status

director	drejtor (m)	[drɛjtór]
superior	epror (m)	[ɛprór]
president	president (m)	[prɛsidént]
assistant	ndihmës (m)	[ndíhməs]
secretary	sekretar (m)	[sɛkrɛtár]

owner, proprietor	pronar (m)	[pronár]
partner	partner (m)	[partnér]
stockholder	aksioner (m)	[aksionér]

businessman	biznesmen (m)	[biznɛsmén]
millionaire	milioner (m)	[milionér]
billionaire	bilioner (m)	[bilionér]

actor	aktor (m)	[aktór]
architect	arkitekt (m)	[arkitékt]
banker	bankier (m)	[bankiér]
broker	komisioner (m)	[komisionér]

veterinarian	veteriner (m)	[vɛtɛrinér]
doctor	mjek (m)	[mjék]
chambermaid	pastruese (f)	[pastrúɛsɛ]
designer	projektues (m)	[projɛktúɛs]
correspondent	korrespondent (m)	[korɛspondént]
delivery man	postier (m)	[postiér]

electrician	elektricist (m)	[ɛlɛktritsíst]
musician	muzikant (m)	[muzikánt]
babysitter	dado (f)	[dádo]
hairdresser	parukiere (f)	[parukiérɛ]
herder, shepherd	bari (m)	[barí]

singer (masc.)	këngëtar (m)	[kəŋətár]
translator	përkthyes (m)	[pərkθýɛs]
writer	shkrimtar (m)	[ʃkrimtár]
carpenter	marangoz (m)	[maraŋóz]
cook	kuzhinier (m)	[kuʒiniér]

fireman	zjarrfikës (m)	[zjarfíkəs]
police officer	polic (m)	[políts]
mailman	postier (m)	[postiér]
programmer	programues (m)	[programúɛs]
salesman (store staff)	shitës (m)	[ʃítəs]

worker	punëtor (m)	[punətór]
gardener	kopshtar (m)	[kopʃtár]
plumber	hidraulik (m)	[hidraulík]

dentist	dentist (m)	[dɛntíst]
flight attendant (fem.)	stjuardesë (f)	[stjuardésə]

dancer (masc.)	valltar (m)	[vaɫtár]
bodyguard	truprojë (f)	[truprójə]

scientist	shkencëtar (m)	[ʃkɛntsətár]
schoolteacher	mësues (m)	[məsúɛs]

farmer	fermer (m)	[fɛrmér]
surgeon	kirurg (m)	[kirúrg]
miner	minator (m)	[minatór]
chef (kitchen chef)	shef kuzhine (m)	[ʃɛf kuʒínɛ]
driver	shofer (m)	[ʃofér]

16. Sport

kind of sports	lloj sporti (m)	[ɫoj spórti]
soccer	futboll (m)	[futbóɫ]
hockey	hokej (m)	[hokéj]
basketball	basketboll (m)	[baskɛtbóɫ]
baseball	bejsboll (m)	[bɛjsbóɫ]

volleyball	volejboll (m)	[volɛjbóɫ]
boxing	boks (m)	[boks]
wrestling	mundje (f)	[múndjɛ]
tennis	tenis (m)	[tɛnís]
swimming	not (m)	[not]

chess	shah (m)	[ʃah]
running	vrapim (m)	[vrapím]
athletics	atletikë (f)	[atlɛtíkə]
figure skating	patinazh (m)	[patináʒ]
cycling	çiklizëm (m)	[tʃiklízəm]

billiards	bilardo (f)	[bilárdo]
bodybuilding	bodybuilding (m)	[bodybuildíŋ]
golf	golf (m)	[golf]
scuba diving	zhytje (f)	[ʒýtjɛ]
sailing	lundrim me vela (m)	[lundrím mɛ véla]
archery	gjuajtje me hark (f)	[ɟúajtjɛ mɛ hárk]

period, half	pjesë (f)	[pjésə]
half-time	pushim (m)	[puʃím]
tie	barazim (m)	[barazím]
to tie (vi)	barazoj	[barazój]

treadmill	makinë vrapi (f)	[makínə vrápi]
player	lojtar (m)	[lojtár]
substitute	zëvendësues (m)	[zəvɛndəsúɛs]
substitutes bench	stol i rezervave (m)	[stol i rɛzérvavɛ]

match	ndeshje (f)	[ndéʃjɛ]
goal	gol (m)	[gol]
goalkeeper	portier (m)	[portiér]
goal (score)	gol (m)	[gol]

Olympic Games	Lojërat Olimpike (pl)	[lójərat olimpíkɛ]
to set a record	vendos rekord	[vɛndós rɛkórd]
final	finale	[finálɛ]
champion	kampion (m)	[kampión]
championship	kampionat (m)	[kampionát]

winner	fitues (m)	[fitúɛs]
victory	fitore (f)	[fitórɛ]
to win (vi)	fitoj	[fitój]

to lose (not win)	humb	[húmb]
medal	medalje (f)	[mɛdáljɛ]

first place	vendi i parë	[véndi i párə]
second place	vendi i dytë	[véndi i dýtə]
third place	vendi i tretë	[véndi i trétə]

stadium	stadium (m)	[stadiúm]
fan, supporter	tifoz (m)	[tifóz]
trainer, coach	trajner (m)	[trajnér]
training	trajnim (m)	[trajním]

17. Foreign languages. Orthography

language	gjuhë (f)	[ɟúhə]
to study (vt)	studioj	[studiój]
pronunciation	shqiptim (m)	[ʃçiptím]
accent	aksent (m)	[aksént]

noun	emër (m)	[émər]
adjective	mbiemër (m)	[mbiémər]
verb	folje (f)	[fóljɛ]
adverb	ndajfolje (f)	[ndajfóljɛ]

pronoun	përemër (m)	[pərémər]
interjection	pasthirrmë (f)	[pasθírmə]
preposition	parafjalë (f)	[parafjálə]

root	rrënjë (f)	[réɲə]
ending	fundore (f)	[fundórɛ]
prefix	parashtesë (f)	[paraʃtésə]
syllable	rrokje (f)	[rókjɛ]
suffix	prapashtesë (f)	[prapaʃtésə]

stress mark	theks (m)	[θɛks]
period, dot	pikë (f)	[píkə]
comma	presje (f)	[présjɛ]
colon	dy pika (f)	[dy píka]
ellipsis	tre pika (f)	[trɛ píka]

question	pyetje (f)	[pýɛtjɛ]
question mark	pikëpyetje (f)	[pikəpýɛtjɛ]
exclamation point	pikëçuditje (f)	[pikətʃudítjɛ]

in quotation marks	në thonjëza	[nə θóɲəza]
in parenthesis	brenda kllapave	[brénda kɬápavɛ]
letter	shkronjë (f)	[ʃkróɲə]
capital letter	shkronjë e madhe (f)	[ʃkróɲə ɛ máðɛ]
sentence	fjali (f)	[fjalí]
group of words	grup fjalësh (m)	[grup fjáləʃ]

expression	shprehje (f)	[ʃpréhjɛ]
subject	kryefjalë (f)	[kryɛfjálə]
predicate	kallëzues (m)	[kałəzúɛs]
line	rresht (m)	[réʃt]
paragraph	paragraf (m)	[paragráf]

synonym	sinonim (m)	[sinoním]
antonym	antonim (m)	[antoním]
exception	përjashtim (m)	[pərjaʃtím]
to underline (vt)	nënvijëzoj	[nənvijəzój]

rules	rregullat (pl)	[régułat]
grammar	gramatikë (f)	[gramatíkə]
vocabulary	fjalor (m)	[fjalór]
phonetics	fonetikë (f)	[fonɛtíkə]
alphabet	alfabet (m)	[alfabét]

textbook	tekst mësimor (m)	[tɛkst məsimór]
dictionary	fjalor (m)	[fjalór]
phrasebook	libër frazeologjik (m)	[líbər frazɛoloʝík]

word	fjalë (f)	[fjálə]
meaning	kuptim (m)	[kuptím]
memory	kujtesë (f)	[kujtésə]

18. The Earth. Geography

the Earth	Toka (f)	[tóka]
the globe (the Earth)	globi (f)	[glóbi]
planet	planet (m)	[planét]

geography	gjeografi (f)	[ʝɛografí]
nature	natyrë (f)	[natýrə]
map	hartë (f)	[hártə]
atlas	atlas (m)	[atlás]

in the north	në veri	[nə vɛrí]
in the south	në jug	[nə jug]
in the west	në perëndim	[nə pɛrəndím]
in the east	në lindje	[nə líndjɛ]

sea	det (m)	[dét]
ocean	oqean (m)	[ocɛán]
gulf (bay)	gji (m)	[ʝi]
straits	ngushticë (f)	[ŋuʃtítsə]

continent (mainland)	kontinent (m)	[kontinént]
island	ishull (m)	[íʃuł]
peninsula	gadishull (m)	[gadíʃuł]
archipelago	arkipelag (m)	[arkipɛlág]

harbor	port (m)	[port]
coral reef	korale nënujorë (f)	[korálɛ nənujórə]
shore	breg (m)	[brɛg]
coast	bregdet (m)	[brɛgdét]

| flow (flood tide) | batica (f) | [batítsa] |
| ebb (ebb tide) | zbaticë (f) | [zbatítsə] |

latitude	gjerësi (f)	[ɟɛrəsí]
longitude	gjatësi (f)	[ɟatəsí]
parallel	paralele (f)	[paralélɛ]
equator	ekuator (m)	[ɛkuatór]

sky	qiell (m)	[cíɛɫ]
horizon	horizont (m)	[horizónt]
atmosphere	atmosferë (f)	[atmosférə]

mountain	mal (m)	[mal]
summit, top	majë (f)	[májə]
cliff	shkëmb (m)	[ʃkəmb]
hill	kodër (f)	[kódər]

volcano	vullkan (m)	[vuɫkán]
glacier	akullnajë (f)	[akuɫnájə]
waterfall	ujëvarë (f)	[ujəvárə]
plain	fushë (f)	[fúʃə]

river	lum (m)	[lum]
spring (natural source)	burim (m)	[burím]
bank (of river)	breg (m)	[brɛg]
downstream (adv)	rrjedhje e poshtme	[rjéðjɛ ɛ póʃtmɛ]
upstream (adv)	rrjedhje e sipërme	[rjéðjɛ ɛ sípərmɛ]

lake	liqen (m)	[licén]
dam	digë (f)	[dígə]
canal	kanal (m)	[kanál]
swamp (marshland)	kënetë (f)	[kənétə]
ice	akull (m)	[ákuɫ]

19. Countries of the world. Part 1

Europe	Evropa (f)	[ɛvrópa]
European Union	Bashkimi Evropian (m)	[baʃkími ɛvropián]
European (n)	Evropian (m)	[ɛvropián]
European (adj)	evropian	[ɛvropián]

Austria	Austri (f)	[austrí]
Great Britain	Britani e Madhe (f)	[brítani ɛ máðɛ]
England	Angli (f)	[aŋlí]
Belgium	Belgjikë (f)	[bɛʎíkə]

Germany	Gjermani (f)	[ɟɛrmaní]
Netherlands	Holandë (f)	[holándə]
Holland	Holandë (f)	[holándə]
Greece	Greqi (f)	[grɛcí]
Denmark	Danimarkë (f)	[danimárkə]
Ireland	Irlandë (f)	[irlándə]

Iceland	Islandë (f)	[islándə]
Spain	Spanjë (f)	[spáɲə]
Italy	Itali (f)	[italí]
Cyprus	Qipro (f)	[cípro]
Malta	Maltë (f)	[máltə]

Norway	Norvegji (f)	[norvɛɟí]
Portugal	Portugali (f)	[portugalí]
Finland	Finlandë (f)	[finlándə]
France	Francë (f)	[frántsə]
Sweden	Suedi (f)	[suɛdí]

Switzerland	Zvicër (f)	[zvítsər]
Scotland	Skoci (f)	[skotsí]
Vatican	Vatikan (m)	[vatikán]
Liechtenstein	Lichtenstein (m)	[litshtɛnstéin]
Luxembourg	Luksemburg (m)	[luksɛmbúrg]

Monaco	Monako (f)	[monáko]
Albania	Shqipëri (f)	[ʃcipərí]
Bulgaria	Bullgari (f)	[buɫgarí]

| Hungary | Hungari (f) | [huɲarí] |
| Latvia | Letoni (f) | [lɛtoní] |

Lithuania	Lituani (f)	[lituaní]
Poland	Poloni (f)	[poloní]
Romania	Rumani (f)	[rumaní]

| Serbia | Serbi (f) | [sɛrbí] |
| Slovakia | Sllovaki (f) | [sɫovakí] |

Croatia	Kroaci (f)	[kroatsí]
Czech Republic	Republika Çeke (f)	[rɛpublíka tʃékɛ]
Estonia	Estoni (f)	[ɛstoní]

| Bosnia and Herzegovina | Bosnje Herzegovina (f) | [bósɲɛ hɛrzɛgovína] |
| Macedonia (Republic of ~) | Maqedonia (f) | [matsɛdonía] |

Slovenia	Sllovenia (f)	[sɫovɛnía]
Montenegro	Mali i Zi (m)	[máli i zí]
Belarus	Bjellorusi (f)	[bjɛɫorusí]
Moldova, Moldavia	Moldavi (f)	[moldaví]
Russia	Rusi (f)	[rusí]
Ukraine	Ukrainë (f)	[ukraínə]

20. Countries of the world. Part 2

Asia	**Azia** (f)	[azía]
Vietnam	**Vietnam** (m)	[viɛtnám]
India	**Indi** (f)	[indí]
Israel	**Izrael** (m)	[izraél]
China	**Kinë** (f)	[kínə]
Lebanon	**Liban** (m)	[libán]
Mongolia	**Mongoli** (f)	[moŋolí]
Malaysia	**Malajzi** (f)	[malajzí]
Pakistan	**Pakistan** (m)	[pakistán]
Saudi Arabia	**Arabia Saudite** (f)	[arabía saudítɛ]
Thailand	**Tajlandë** (f)	[tajlándə]
Taiwan	**Tajvan** (m)	[tajván]
Turkey	**Turqi** (f)	[turcí]
Japan	**Japoni** (f)	[japoní]
Afghanistan	**Afganistan** (m)	[afganistán]
Bangladesh	**Bangladesh** (m)	[baŋladéʃ]
Indonesia	**Indonezi** (f)	[indonɛzí]
Jordan	**Jordani** (f)	[jordaní]
Iraq	**Irak** (m)	[irak]
Iran	**Iran** (m)	[irán]
Cambodia	**Kamboxhia** (f)	[kambódʒia]
Kuwait	**Kuvajt** (m)	[kuvájt]
Laos	**Laos** (m)	[láos]
Myanmar	**Mianmar** (m)	[mianmáɾ]
Nepal	**Nepal** (m)	[nɛpál]
United Arab Emirates	**Emiratet e Bashkuara Arabe** (pl)	[ɛmirátɛt ɛ baʃkúara arábɛ]
Syria	**Siri** (f)	[sirí]
Palestine	**Palestinë** (f)	[palɛstínə]
South Korea	**Korea e Jugut** (f)	[koréa ɛ júgut]
North Korea	**Korea e Veriut** (f)	[koréa ɛ vériut]
United States of America	**Shtetet e Bashkuara të Amerikës**	[ʃtétɛt ɛ baʃkúara tə amɛríkəs]
Canada	**Kanada** (f)	[kanadá]
Mexico	**Meksikë** (f)	[mɛksíkə]
Argentina	**Argjentinë** (f)	[aɾɟɛntínə]
Brazil	**Brazil** (m)	[brazíl]
Colombia	**Kolumbi** (f)	[kolumbí]
Cuba	**Kuba** (f)	[kúba]
Chile	**Kili** (m)	[kíli]
Venezuela	**Venezuelë** (f)	[vɛnɛzuélə]
Ecuador	**Ekuador** (m)	[ɛkuadóɾ]

The Bahamas	Bahamas (m)	[bahámas]
Panama	Panama (f)	[panamá]
Egypt	Egjipt (m)	[ɛɟípt]
Morocco	Marok (m)	[marók]
Tunisia	Tunizi (f)	[tunizí]

Kenya	Kenia (f)	[kénia]
Libya	Libia (f)	[libía]
South Africa	Afrika e Jugut (f)	[afríka ɛ júgut]
Australia	Australia (f)	[australía]
New Zealand	Zelandë e Re (f)	[zɛlándə ɛ ré]

21. Weather. Natural disasters

weather	moti (m)	[móti]
weather forecast	parashikimi i motit (m)	[paraʃikími i mótit]
temperature	temperaturë (f)	[tɛmpɛratúrə]
thermometer	termometër (m)	[tɛrmométər]
barometer	barometër (m)	[barométər]

sun	diell (m)	[díɛɫ]
to shine (vi)	ndriçon	[ndritʃón]
sunny (day)	me diell	[mɛ díɛɫ]
to come up (vi)	agon	[agón]
to set (vi)	perëndon	[pɛrəndón]

rain	shi (m)	[ʃi]
it's raining	bie shi	[bíɛ ʃi]
pouring rain	shi litar (m)	[ʃi litár]
rain cloud	re shiu (f)	[rɛ ʃiu]
puddle	brakë (f)	[brákə]
to get wet (in rain)	lagem	[lágɛm]

thunderstorm	stuhi (f)	[stuhí]
lightning (~ strike)	vetëtimë (f)	[vɛtətímə]
to flash (vi)	vetëton	[vɛtətón]
thunder	bubullimë (f)	[bubuɫímə]
it's thundering	bubullon	[bubuɫón]
hail	breshër (m)	[bréʃər]
it's hailing	po bie breshër	[po bíɛ bréʃər]

heat (extreme ~)	vapë (f)	[vápə]
it's hot	është nxehtë	[əʃtə ndzéhtə]
it's warm	është ngrohtë	[əʃtə ŋróhtə]
it's cold	bën ftohtë	[bən ftóhtə]

fog (mist)	mjegull (f)	[mjéguɫ]
foggy	e mjegullt	[ɛ mjéguɫt]
cloud	re (f)	[rɛ]
cloudy (adj)	vranët	[vránət]

humidity	lagështi (f)	[lagəʃtí]
snow	borë (f)	[bórə]
it's snowing	bie borë	[bíɛ bórə]
frost (severe ~, freezing cold)	ngricë (f)	[ŋrítsə]
below zero (adv)	nën zero	[nən zéro]
hoarfrost	brymë (f)	[brýmə]

bad weather	mot i keq (m)	[mot i kɛc]
disaster	fatkeqësi (f)	[fatkɛcəsí]
flood, inundation	përmbytje (f)	[pərmbýtjɛ]
avalanche	ortek (m)	[orték]
earthquake	tërmet (m)	[tərmét]

tremor, shoke	lëkundje (f)	[ləkúndjɛ]
epicenter	epiqendër (f)	[ɛpicéndər]
eruption	shpërthim (m)	[ʃpərθím]
lava	llavë (f)	[ɫávə]

tornado	tornado (f)	[tornádo]
twister	vorbull (f)	[vórbuɫ]
hurricane	uragan (m)	[uragán]
tsunami	cunam (m)	[tsunám]
cyclone	ciklon (m)	[tsiklón]

22. Animals. Part 1

animal	kafshë (f)	[káʃʃə]
predator	grabitqar (m)	[grabitcár]

tiger	tigër (m)	[tígər]
lion	luan (m)	[luán]
wolf	ujk (m)	[ujk]
fox	dhelpër (f)	[ðélpər]
jaguar	jaguar (m)	[jaguár]

lynx	rrëqebull (m)	[rəcébuɫ]
coyote	kojotë (f)	[kojótə]
jackal	çakall (m)	[tʃakáɫ]
hyena	hienë (f)	[hiénə]

squirrel	ketër (m)	[kétər]
hedgehog	iriq (m)	[iríc]
rabbit	lepur (m)	[lépur]
raccoon	rakun (m)	[rakún]

hamster	hamster (m)	[hamstér]
mole	urith (m)	[uríθ]
mouse	mi (m)	[mi]
rat	mi (m)	[mi]

bat	lakuriq (m)	[lakuríc]
beaver	kastor (m)	[kastór]
horse	kali (m)	[káli]
deer	dre (f)	[drɛ]
camel	deve (f)	[dévɛ]
zebra	zebër (f)	[zébər]

whale	balenë (f)	[balénə]
seal	fokë (f)	[fókə]
walrus	lopë deti (f)	[lópə déti]
dolphin	delfin (m)	[dɛlfín]

bear	ari (m)	[arí]
monkey	majmun (m)	[majmún]
elephant	elefant (m)	[ɛlɛfánt]
rhinoceros	rinoqeront (m)	[rinocɛrónt]
giraffe	gjirafë (f)	[ɟiráfə]

hippopotamus	hipopotam (m)	[hipopotám]
kangaroo	kangur (m)	[kaŋúr]
cat	mace (f)	[mátsɛ]
dog	qen (m)	[cɛn]

cow	lopë (f)	[lópə]
bull	dem (m)	[dém]
sheep (ewe)	dele (f)	[délɛ]
goat	dhi (f)	[ði]

donkey	gomar (m)	[gomár]
pig, hog	derr (m)	[dɛr]
hen (chicken)	pulë (f)	[púlə]
rooster	gjel (m)	[ɟél]

duck	rosë (f)	[rósə]
goose	patë (f)	[pátə]
turkey (hen)	gjel deti (m)	[ɟél déti]
sheepdog	qen dhensh (m)	[cɛn ðɛnʃ]

23. Animals. Part 2

bird	zog (m)	[zog]
pigeon	pëllumb (m)	[pəɫúmb]
sparrow	harabel (m)	[harabél]
tit (great tit)	xhixhimës (m)	[dʒidʒimés]
magpie	laraskë (f)	[laráskə]

eagle	shqiponjë (f)	[ʃcipóɲə]
hawk	gjeraqinë (f)	[ɟɛracínə]
falcon	fajkua (f)	[fajkúa]
swan	mjellmë (f)	[mjéɫmə]

crane	lejlek (m)	[lɛjlék]
stork	lejlek (m)	[lɛjlék]
parrot	papagall (m)	[papagáł]
peacock	pallua (m)	[patúa]
ostrich	struc (m)	[struts]
heron	çafkë (f)	[tʃáfkə]
nightingale	bilbil (m)	[bilbíl]
swallow	dallëndyshe (f)	[datəndýʃɛ]
woodpecker	qukapik (m)	[cukapík]
cuckoo	kukuvajkë (f)	[kukuvájkə]
owl	buf (m)	[buf]
penguin	penguin (m)	[pɛŋuín]
tuna	tunë (f)	[túnə]
trout	troftë (f)	[tróftə]
eel	ngjalë (f)	[nɟálə]
shark	peshkaqen (m)	[pɛʃkacén]
crab	gaforre (f)	[gafórɛ]
jellyfish	kandil deti (m)	[kandíl déti]
octopus	oktapod (m)	[oktapód]
starfish	yll deti (m)	[yt déti]
sea urchin	iriq deti (m)	[iríc déti]
seahorse	kalë deti (m)	[kálə déti]
shrimp	karkalec (m)	[karkaléts]
snake	gjarpër (m)	[ɟárpər]
viper	nepërka (f)	[nɛpérka]
lizard	hardhucë (f)	[harðútsə]
iguana	iguana (f)	[iguána]
chameleon	kameleon (m)	[kamɛlɛón]
scorpion	akrep (m)	[akrép]
turtle	breshkë (f)	[bréʃkə]
frog	bretkosë (f)	[brɛtkósə]
crocodile	krokodil (m)	[krokodíl]
insect, bug	insekt (m)	[insékt]
butterfly	flutur (f)	[flútur]
ant	milingonë (f)	[miliŋónə]
fly	mizë (f)	[mízə]
mosquito	mushkonjë (f)	[muʃkóɲə]
beetle	brumbull (m)	[brúmbuł]
bee	bletë (f)	[blétə]
spider	merimangë (f)	[mɛrimáŋə]

24. Trees. Plants

tree	pemë (f)	[pémə]
birch	mështekna (f)	[məʃtékna]
oak	lis (m)	[lis]
linden tree	bli (m)	[blí]
aspen	plep i egër (m)	[plɛp i égər]

maple	panjë (f)	[páɲə]
spruce	bredh (m)	[brɛð]
pine	pishë (f)	[píʃə]
cedar	kedër (m)	[kédər]

poplar	plep (m)	[plɛp]
rowan	vadhë (f)	[váðə]
beech	ah (m)	[ah]
elm	elm (m)	[élm]

ash (tree)	shelg (m)	[ʃɛlg]
chestnut	gështenjë (f)	[gəʃtéɲə]
palm tree	palma (f)	[pálma]
bush	shkurre (f)	[ʃkúrɛ]

mushroom	kërpudhë (f)	[kərpúðə]
poisonous mushroom	kërpudhë helmuese (f)	[kərpúðə hɛlmúɛsɛ]
cep (Boletus edulis)	porcini (m)	[portsíni]
russula	rusula (f)	[rúsula]
fly agaric	kësulkuqe (f)	[kəsulkúcɛ]
death cap	kërpudha e vdekjes (f)	[kərpúða ɛ vdékjɛs]

flower	lule (f)	[lúlɛ]
bouquet (of flowers)	buqetë (f)	[bucétə]
rose (flower)	trëndafil (m)	[trəndafíl]
tulip	tulipan (m)	[tulipán]
carnation	karafil (m)	[karafíl]

camomile	kamomil (m)	[kamomíl]
cactus	kaktus (m)	[kaktús]
lily of the valley	zambak i fushës (m)	[zambák i fúʃəs]
snowdrop	luleborë (f)	[lulɛbórə]
water lily	zambak uji (m)	[zambák új i]

conservatory (greenhouse)	serrë (f)	[sérə]
lawn	lëndinë (f)	[ləndínə]
flowerbed	kënd lulishteje (m)	[kənd lulíʃtɛjɛ]

plant	bimë (f)	[bímə]
grass	bar (m)	[barɾ]
leaf	gjeth (m)	[ɟɛθ]
petal	petale (f)	[pɛtálɛ]
stem	bisht (m)	[biʃt]

young plant (shoot)	**filiz** (m)	[filíz]
cereal crops	**drithëra** (pl)	[dríθəra]
wheat	**grurë** (f)	[grúrə]
rye	**thekër** (f)	[θékər]
oats	**tërshërë** (f)	[tərʃérə]

millet	**mel** (m)	[mɛl]
barley	**elb** (m)	[ɛlb]
corn	**misër** (m)	[mísər]
rice	**oriz** (m)	[oríz]

25. Various useful words

balance (of situation)	**ekuilibër** (m)	[ɛkuilíbər]
base (basis)	**bazë** (f)	[bázə]
beginning	**fillim** (m)	[fitím]
category	**kategori** (f)	[katɛgorí]

choice	**zgjedhje** (f)	[zɟéðjɛ]
coincidence	**rastësi** (f)	[rastəsí]
comparison	**krahasim** (m)	[krahasím]
degree (extent, amount)	**nivel** (m)	[nivél]

development	**zhvillim** (m)	[ʒvitím]
difference	**ndryshim** (m)	[ndryʃím]
effect (e.g., of drugs)	**efekt** (m)	[ɛfékt]
effort (exertion)	**përpjekje** (f)	[pərpjékjɛ]

element	**element** (m)	[ɛlɛmént]
example (illustration)	**shembull** (m)	[ʃémbuɫ]
fact	**fakt** (m)	[fakt]
help	**ndihmë** (f)	[ndíhmə]

ideal	**ideal** (m)	[idɛál]
kind (sort, type)	**lloj** (m)	[ɫoj]
mistake, error	**gabim** (m)	[gabím]
moment	**moment** (m)	[mománt]

obstacle	**pengesë** (f)	[pɛɲésə]
part (~ of sth)	**pjesë** (f)	[pjésə]
pause (break)	**pushim** (m)	[puʃím]
position	**pozicion** (m)	[pozitsión]

problem	**problem** (m)	[problém]
process	**proces** (m)	[protsés]
progress	**ecje përpara** (f)	[étsjɛ pərpára]
property (quality)	**cilësi** (f)	[tsiləsí]
reaction	**reagim** (m)	[rɛagím]
risk	**rrezik** (m)	[rɛzík]

secret	sekret (m)	[sɛkrét]
series	seri (f)	[sɛrí]
shape (outer form)	formë (f)	[fórmə]
situation	situatë (f)	[situátə]
solution	zgjidhje (f)	[zɟíðjɛ]
standard (adj)	standard	[standárd]
stop (pause)	pauzë (f)	[paúzə]
style	stil (m)	[stil]
system	sistem (m)	[sistém]
table (chart)	tabelë (f)	[tabélə]
tempo, rate	ritëm (m)	[rítəm]
term (word, expression)	term (m)	[tɛrm]
truth (e.g., moment of ~)	e vërtetë (f)	[ɛ vərtétə]
turn (please wait your ~)	kthesë (f)	[kθésə]
urgent (adj)	urgjent	[urɲént]
utility (usefulness)	vegël (f)	[végəl]
variant (alternative)	variant (m)	[variánt]
way (means, method)	rrugëzgjidhje (f)	[rugəzɟíðjɛ]
zone	zonë (f)	[zónə]

26. Modifiers. Adjectives. Part 1

additional (adj)	shtesë	[ʃtésə]
ancient (~ civilization)	i lashtë	[i láʃtə]
artificial (adj)	artificial	[artifitsiál]
bad (adj)	i keq	[i kéc]
beautiful (person)	i bukur	[i búkur]
big (in size)	i madh	[i máð]
bitter (taste)	i hidhur	[i híður]
blind (sightless)	i verbër	[i vérbər]
central (adj)	qendror	[cɛndrór]
children's (adj)	i fëmijëve	[i fəmíjəvɛ]
clandestine (secret)	klandestin	[klandɛstín]
clean (free from dirt)	i pastër	[i pástər]
clever (smart)	i zgjuar	[i zɟúar]
compatible (adj)	i përshtatshëm	[i pərʃtátʃəm]
contented (satisfied)	i kënaqur	[i kənácur]
dangerous (adj)	i rrezikshëm	[i rɛzíkʃəm]
dead (not alive)	i vdekur	[i vdékur]
dense (fog, smoke)	i dendur	[i déndur]
difficult (decision)	i vështirë	[i vəʃtírə]
dirty (not clean)	i pistë	[i pístə]
easy (not difficult)	i lehtë	[i léhtə]

empty (glass, room)	zbrazët	[zbrázət]
exact (amount)	i saktë	[i sáktə]
excellent (adj)	i shkëlqyer	[i ʃkəlcýɛr]

excessive (adj)	i tepërt	[i tépərt]
exterior (adj)	i jashtëm	[i jáʃtəm]
fast (quick)	i shpejtë	[i ʃpéjtə]
fertile (land, soil)	pjellore	[pjɛtórɛ]
fragile (china, glass)	delikat	[dɛlikát]

free (at no cost)	falas	[fálas]
fresh (~ water)	i freskët	[i fréskət]
frozen (food)	i ngrirë	[i ŋrírə]
full (completely filled)	i mbushur	[i mbúʃur]
happy (adj)	i lumtur	[i lúmtur]

hard (not soft)	i fortë	[i fórtə]
huge (adj)	i madh	[i máð]
ill (sick, unwell)	i sëmurë	[i səmúrə]
immobile (adj)	i palëvizshëm	[i paləvízʃəm]
important (adj)	i rëndësishëm	[i rəndəsíʃəm]

interior (adj)	i brendshëm	[i bréndʃəm]
last (e.g., ~ week)	i fundit	[i fúndit]
last (final)	i fundit	[i fúndit]
left (e.g., ~ side)	majtë	[májtə]
legal (legitimate)	ligjor	[liɟór]

light (in weight)	i lehtë	[i léhtə]
liquid (fluid)	i lëngët	[i lə́ŋət]
long (e.g., ~ hair)	i gjatë	[i ɟátə]
loud (voice, etc.)	i lartë	[i lártə]
low (voice)	i ulët	[i úlət]

27. Modifiers. Adjectives. Part 2

main (principal)	kryesor	[kryɛsór]
matt, matte	mat	[mat]
mysterious (adj)	misterioz	[mistɛrióz]
narrow (street, etc.)	i ngushtë	[i ŋúʃtə]
native (~ country)	autokton	[autoktón]

negative (~ response)	negativ	[nɛgatív]
new (adj)	i ri	[i rí]
next (e.g., ~ week)	tjetër	[tjétər]
normal (adj)	normal	[normál]
not difficult (adj)	jo i vështirë	[jo i vəʃtírə]

obligatory (adj)	i detyrueshëm	[i dɛtyrúɛʃəm]
old (house)	i vjetër	[i vjétər]

open (adj)	i hapur	[i hápur]
opposite (adj)	i kundërt	[i kúndərt]
ordinary (usual)	i zakonshëm	[i zakónʃəm]

original (unusual)	origjinal	[oriɟinál]
personal (adj)	personal	[pɛrsonál]
polite (adj)	i sjellshëm	[i sjétʃəm]
poor (not rich)	i varfër	[i várfər]
possible (adj)	i mundur	[i múndur]
principal (main)	kryesor	[kryɛsór]
probable (adj)	i mundshëm	[i múndʃəm]
prolonged (e.g., ~ applause)	i zgjatur	[i zɟátur]
public (open to all)	publik	[publík]

rare (adj)	i rrallë	[i rátə]
raw (uncooked)	i gjallë	[i ɟátə]
right (not left)	djathtë	[djáθtə]
ripe (fruit)	i pjekur	[i pjékur]

risky (adj)	i rrezikshëm	[i rɛzíkʃəm]
sad (~ look)	i mërzitur	[i mərzítur]
second hand (adj)	i përdorur	[i pərdórur]
shallow (water)	i cekët	[i tsékət]
sharp (blade, etc.)	i mprehtë	[i mpréhtə]
short (in length)	i shkurtër	[i ʃkúrtər]
similar (adj)	i ngjashëm	[i nɟáʃəm]
small (in size)	i vogël	[i vógəl]
smooth (surface)	i lëmuar	[i ləmúar]
soft (~ toys)	i butë	[i bútə]

solid (~ wall)	i ngjeshur	[i nɟéʃur]
sour (flavor, taste)	i hidhur	[i híður]
spacious (house, etc.)	i bollshëm	[i bótʃəm]
special (adj)	i veçantë	[i vɛtʃántə]

straight (line, road)	i drejtë	[i dréjtə]
strong (person)	i fortë	[i fórtə]
stupid (foolish)	budalla	[budatá]
superb, perfect (adj)	i përsosur	[i pərsósur]

sweet (sugary)	i ëmbël	[i émbəl]
tan (adj)	i nxirë	[i ndzírə]
tasty (delicious)	i shijshëm	[i ʃíjʃəm]
unclear (adj)	i paqartë	[i pacártə]

28. Verbs. Part 1

| to accuse (vt) | akuzoj | [akuzój] |
| to agree (say yes) | bie dakord | [bíɛ dakórd] |

107

to announce (vt)	njoftoj	[ɲoftój]
to answer (vi, vt)	përgjigjem	[pəɾɟíɟɛm]
to apologize (vi)	kërkoj falje	[kərkój fáljɛ]

to arrive (vi)	arrij	[aríj]
to ask (~ oneself)	pyes	[pýɛs]
to be absent	mungoj	[muŋój]
to be afraid	kam frikë	[kam fríkə]
to be born	lind	[lind]

to be in a hurry	nxitoj	[ndzitój]
to beat (to hit)	rrah	[rah]
to begin (vt)	filloj	[fiɫój]
to believe (in God)	besoj	[bɛsój]
to belong to ...	përkas ...	[pərkás ...]
to break (split into pieces)	ndahem	[ndáhɛm]

to build (vt)	ndërtoj	[ndərtój]
to buy (purchase)	blej	[blɛj]
can (v aux)	mund	[mund]
can (v aux)	mund	[mund]
to cancel (call off)	anuloj	[anulój]

to catch (vt)	kap	[kap]
to change (vt)	ndryshoj	[ndryʃój]
to check (to examine)	kontrolloj	[kontroɫój]
to choose (select)	zgjedh	[zɟɛð]
to clean up (tidy)	rregulloj	[rɛguɫój]

to close (vt)	mbyll	[mbyɫ]
to compare (vt)	krahasoj	[krahasój]
to complain (vi, vt)	ankohem	[ankóhɛm]
to confirm (vt)	konfirmoj	[konfirmój]
to congratulate (vt)	përgëzoj	[pərgəzój]

to cook (dinner)	gatuaj	[gatúaj]
to copy (vt)	kopjoj	[kopjój]
to cost (vt)	kushton	[kuʃtón]
to count (add up)	numëroj	[numərój]
to count on ...	mbështetem ...	[mbəʃtétɛm ...]

to create (vt)	krijoj	[krijój]
to cry (weep)	qaj	[caj]
to dance (vi, vt)	vallëzoj	[vaɫəzój]
to deceive (vi, vt)	mashtroj	[maʃtrój]
to decide (~ to do sth)	vendos	[vɛndós]

to delete (vt)	fshij	[fʃij]
to demand (request firmly)	kërkoj	[kərkój]
to deny (vt)	mohoj	[mohój]
to depend on ...	varem nga ...	[várɛm ŋa ...]
to despise (vt)	përbuz	[pərbúz]

to die (vi)	vdes	[vdɛs]
to dig (vt)	gërmoj	[gərmój]
to disappear (vi)	zhduk	[ʒduk]
to discuss (vt)	diskutoj	[diskutój]
to disturb (vt)	shqetësoj	[ʃcɛtəsój]

29. Verbs. Part 2

to dive (vi)	zhytem	[ʒýtɛm]
to divorce (vi)	divorcoj	[divortsój]
to do (vt)	bëj	[bəj]
to doubt (have doubts)	dyshoj	[dyʃój]
to drink (vi, vt)	pi	[pi]

to drop (let fall)	lëshoj	[ləʃój]
to dry (clothes, hair)	thaj	[θaj]
to eat (vi, vt)	ha	[ha]
to end (~ a relationship)	përfundoj	[pərfundój]
to excuse (forgive)	fal	[fal]

to exist (vi)	ekzistoj	[ɛkzistój]
to expect (foresee)	parashikoj	[paraʃikój]
to explain (vt)	shpjegoj	[ʃpjɛgój]
to fall (vi)	bie	[bíɛ]
to fight (street fight, etc.)	grindem	[gríndɛm]
to find (vt)	gjej	[ɟéj]

to finish (vt)	përfundoj	[pərfundój]
to fly (vi)	fluturoj	[fluturój]
to forbid (vt)	ndaloj	[ndalój]
to forget (vi, vt)	harroj	[harój]
to forgive (vt)	fal	[fal]

to get tired	lodhem	[lóðɛm]
to give (vt)	jap	[jap]
to go (on foot)	ec në këmbë	[ɛts nə kémbə]
to hate (vt)	urrej	[uréj]

to have (vt)	kam	[kam]
to have breakfast	ha mëngjes	[ha mənɟés]
to have dinner	ha darkë	[ha dárkə]
to have lunch	ha drekë	[ha drékə]

to hear (vt)	dëgjoj	[dəɟój]
to help (vt)	ndihmoj	[ndihmój]
to hide (vt)	fsheh	[fʃéh]
to hope (vi, vt)	shpresoj	[ʃprɛsój]
to hunt (vi, vt)	dal për gjah	[dál pər ɟáh]
to hurry (vi)	nxitoj	[ndzitój]
to insist (vi, vt)	këmbëngul	[kəmbəŋúl]

to insult (vt)	fyej	[fýɛj]
to invite (vt)	ftoj	[ftoj]
to joke (vi)	bëj shaka	[bəj ʃaká]
to keep (vt)	mbaj	[mbáj]

to kill (vt)	vras	[vras]
to know (sb)	njoh	[ɲóh]
to know (sth)	di	[di]
to like (I like …)	pëlqej	[pəlcéj]
to look at …	shikoj …	[ʃikój …]

to lose (umbrella, etc.)	humb	[húmb]
to love (sb)	dashuroj	[daʃurój]
to make a mistake	gaboj	[gabój]
to meet (vi, vt)	takoj	[takój]
to miss (school, etc.)	humbas	[humbás]

30. Verbs. Part 3

to obey (vi, vt)	bindem	[bíndɛm]
to open (vt)	hap	[hap]
to participate (vi)	marr pjesë	[mar pjésə]
to pay (vi, vt)	paguaj	[pagúaj]
to permit (vt)	lejoj	[lɛjój]

to play (children)	luaj	[lúaj]
to pray (vi, vt)	lutem	[lútɛm]
to promise (vt)	premtoj	[prɛmtój]
to propose (vt)	propozoj	[propozój]
to prove (vt)	dëshmoj	[dəʃmój]
to read (vi, vt)	lexoj	[lɛdzój]

to receive (vt)	pranoj	[pranój]
to rent (sth from sb)	marr me qira	[mar mɛ cirá]
to repeat (say again)	përsëris	[pərsərís]
to reserve, to book	rezervoj	[rɛzɛrvój]
to run (vi)	vrapoj	[vrapój]

to save (rescue)	shpëtoj	[ʃpətój]
to say (~ thank you)	them	[θɛm]
to see (vt)	shikoj	[ʃikój]
to sell (vt)	shes	[ʃɛs]
to send (vt)	dërgoj	[dərgój]
to shoot (vi)	qëlloj	[cətój]

to shout (vi)	bërtas	[bərtás]
to show (vt)	tregoj	[trɛgój]
to sign (document)	nënshkruaj	[nənʃkrúaj]
to sing (vi)	këndoj	[kəndój]
to sit down (vi)	ulem	[úlɛm]

to smile (vi)	buzëqesh	[buzəcéʃ]
to speak (vi, vt)	flas	[flas]
to steal (money, etc.)	vjedh	[vjɛð]
to stop	ndaloj	[ndalój]
(please ~ calling me)		
to study (vt)	studioj	[studiój]
to swim (vi)	notoj	[notój]
to take (vt)	marr	[mar]
to talk to ...	bisedoj ...	[bisɛdój ...]
to tell (story, joke)	tregoj	[trɛgój]
to thank (vt)	falënderoj	[faləndɛrój]
to think (vi, vt)	mendoj	[mɛndój]
to translate (vt)	përkthej	[pərkθéj]
to trust (vt)	besoj	[bɛsój]
to try (attempt)	përpiqem	[pərpícɛm]
to turn (e.g., ~ left)	kthej	[kθɛj]
to turn off	fik	[fik]
to turn on	ndez	[ndɛz]
to understand (vt)	kuptoj	[kuptój]
to wait (vt)	pres	[prɛs]
to want (wish, desire)	dëshiroj	[dəʃirój]
to work (vi)	punoj	[punój]
to write (vt)	shkruaj	[ʃkrúaj]

Made in the USA
Coppell, TX
11 December 2022

88575851R00063